ORIGINS OF THE BRITISH ISRAELITES

The Lost Tribes

ORIGINS OF THE BRITISH ISRAELITES

The Lost Tribes

O. Michael Friedman

Mellen Research University Press
San Francisco

DS
131
.F75
1993

Library of Congress Cataloging-in-Publication Data

Friedman, O. Michael (Oscar Michael), 1918-
    Origins of the British Israelites : the lost tribes / O. Michael
Friedman.
      p.   cm.
    Includes bibliographical references.
    ISBN 0-7734-2306-0
    1. Anglo-Israelism. I. Title.
DS131.F75   1993
941' .004924--dc20   92-42338
                                                        CIP

Editorial Inquiries:

Mellen Research University Press
534 Pacific Avenue
San Francisco
CA 94133

Order Fulfillment:

The Edwin Mellen Press
P.O. Box 450
Lewiston, NY 14092
USA

Printed in the United States of America

To my son Michael and daughter Francine Kammel and to my loving, faithful and patient wife, I dedicate this book. Chic has been my faithful companion for forty-eight years. She truly has been a help mate. "Who shall find a virtuous woman? For such a one is more valuable than precious stones" (Prov. 31:10).

TABLE OF CONTENTS

ACKNOWLEDGEMENTS

Sincere appreciation is expressed to those who have given aid and encouragement in the preparation of this dissertation: Dr. Kenneth Leetsma, my advisor; Mrs. Laura Newton, in the typing of my first draft; Mr. Hal Fritchen, for his close supervision with the writer in this work; Dr. Herman Hoeh, for his original sources of the British-Israelism movement; a friend of thirty-five years, Mr. John Hutton, who, to my surprise, is a British-Israelite, and who supplied me with books as well as periodicals.

It is the prayer of this writer that this dissertation will be a help to those honestly seeking the truth and trust that it might bring honor and glory to "God, even the Father of our Lord Jesus Christ" (2 Cor. 1:3).

Chapter 1

Introduction

THE PROBLEM TO BE FACED

The apparent misconceptions and mysteries as to the claims that British Israelites are the Ten Lost Tribes of Israel challenged the writer to present this dissertation.

There is a great deal of confusion as to the whereabouts of the Twelve Tribes of Israel. Various groups claim they are the Twelve Tribes of Israel, or part of them. British Israelites unreservedly state that they are the Ten Lost Tribes of Israel. Statements like these need clarification. Some schools of thought teach that the Twelve Tribes of Israel have been disbanded by God and dispersed into all peoples.

It is the desire of this writer, through this investigation, to answer many of the questions that previously have appeared unanswerable. This investigation also will be helpful to pastors ministering in the western part of the United States in order to shed light on a major religious body which has a wide following.

BACKGROUND OF THE STUDY

Biblical tradition holds that the Twelve Tribes of Israel descended from the sons and grandsons of Jacob (Gen. 29-30, 35-16-18, 48:4-5, 49).

The Twelve Tribes of Israel are an ancient designation for the Hebrew people, who, after the death of Moses, took possession of the Promised Land of Canaan under the leadership of Joshua. Because the tribes were named after sons or grandsons of Jacob, the Hebrew people became known as Israelites. Jacob's first wife, Leah, bore him six sons: Reuben, Simeon, Levi, Judah, Issachar and Zebulun. With the exception of Levi, each was the father of a tribe. Two other tribes, Gad and Asher, were named after sons born to Jacob and Zilpah, Leah's maidservant. Two additional tribes, Dan and Naphtali, were named after sons of Jacob born of Bilhah, the maidservant of Rachel, Jacob's second wife. Rachel bore Jacob two sons, Joseph and Benjamin, but no tribe bore the name of Joseph. Two tribes, however, were named after Joseph's sons, Manasseh and Ephraim.

Israel entered history as a covenant society. For some two hundred years after her first appearance in Palestine, she had no statehood, no organization as far as government went, no administration and above all, no king. She was a sacral league of tribes united in covenant with Yahweh.

It was the will of God that united the tribes one to another and made them a people with a strong sense of solidarity. It was in the name of Yahweh, and in the covenant sanctioned by Yahweh, that the tribes found this unifying bond.

It was under the theocratic monarchy established by David that the twelve tribes were welded into a united and powerful nation which should have continued (1 Kings 6:11-13), but because the people turned from God's commandments and statutes, God warned Solomon that He would "cut off Israel out of the land," destroy the sanctuary, and make "Israel a proverb and byword among the people" (1 Kings 9:4-7, 11: 11-13). The ten tribes, which separated from the house of David after Solomon's death, soon showed their preference for idol-worship instead of the worship of God in the temple at Jerusalem.

IMPORTANCE OF THE STUDY

1. There are a number of important major religious movements in the Western United States that command the allegiance of millions of citizens. One of their major appeals is the claim of being one of the Lost Tribes of Israel.

2. A study of this nature will help Christian workers in the west better understand those religious groups which claim to be related to the Lost Tribes of Israel.

3. Such a study will shed light on a basic appeal of groups such as the British-Israelism movement; namely, their ability to convince followers that by joining their movement, they will be recipients of the blessings promised to Israel and be able to understand how those blessings belong to America.

4. A reader of this dissertation will have a better understanding of how movements, like the British-Israelism Movement, have formulated religious beliefs which enable followers to believe that they belong to a religion which is at the same time the most American and the most Jewish of all contemporary religions.

STATEMENT OF THE PROBLEM

Very briefly, the Anglo-Israel position is that the Anglo-Saxon peoples, especially Great Britain and the United States, are descended from the tribes of Israel of the Northern Kingdom, and therefore inherit the promises and responsibilities addressed in the Scriptures to Israel. *The National Message*, the official journal of the British-Israel World Federation, introduces its articles with these words:

"The following should be read in the light of Israel Truth - namely, that the Anglo-Saxon nation; the inheritors of her Charters, the possessors of her guarantees and immunities from destruction, the executors of her commissions, are the descendants of Israel."[1]

In light of this statement, the veracity of these claims deserves investigation.

PURPOSE OF THE STUDY

The purpose of this dissertation will be to formulate a synthesis of the views of British-Israelism followed by an investigation of their claims. Having accomplished this, the remainder of this paper will be a refutation of the claims of British-Israelism and the value of this study for Evangelical Christianity.

QUESTIONS TO BE ANSWERED

1. What are the views embraced by the British-Israelism Movement regarding its relationship to the Ten Lost Tribes of Israel?
2. Why is an understanding of these views essential to the understanding of the broader movement itself?
3. How do these views contribute to the appeal of movements such as British-Israelism?
4. How does the British-Israelism Movement view its relationship to the histories of Israel and the United States?

LIMITATIONS OF THE STUDY

1. It is not the purpose of this study to discuss a general investigation of the Lost Tribes of Israel or eschatology.
2. Although this study will shed light on religious groups which claim to be associated with the Lost Tribes, it will not be a general study of the numerous groups which make such claims.
3. This study will not deal in depth with the historical evolution of the British-Israelism Movement. The study will be limited to their views as they exist in the twentieth century.

4. The intention of this dissertation is to look at the views, test them by Scripture, and draw conclusions based upon these examinations.

ORGANIZATION OF THE STUDY

The rest of this study is presented in the following manner. For an overview of the study, a "Table of Contents" is provided in front of this dissertation.

Chapter 2 presents the historical setting of the twelve tribes and their movement from a monarchy to their captivity. Reference is then made into the Ten Lost Tribes Theory, which then brings us into the British-Israelism Movement, their origin, founders by name of this movement, and the leading proponent of this theory in the United States.

Chapter 3 presents the claims of British-Israelism.

Chapter 4 presents a refutation to the above claims.

Chapter 5 describes the dangers of the British Israelite Movement.

Chapter 6 will show the value of this study for evangelical Christianity in the twentieth century and a direction for pastors in the western part of the United States.

Chapter 7 will summarize the findings and draw the conclusions of this study.

The Bibliography and Appendices will follow the final chapter.

ENDNOTES

1   *The National Message* [London], Vol. 59, No. 1688 (July, 1980), p. 108.

CHAPTER 2

THE HISTORICAL SETTING

INTRODUCTION

Before an intelligent investigation can be initiated and presented, one must touch on the historical background of our study. Following the historical background, some insights into the Ten Lost Tribes Theory must be presented. The origin of British-Israelism and its modern proponents and the leading proponent in America today are of great importance to set the stage for this investigation.

THE TWELVE TRIBES OF ISRAEL

The Hebrew word "shevet" (שֵׁבֶט) is translated in our English Bible by the words, "red," "scepter," "staff," "tribe." The initial usage of this word is found in Genesis 49:10, "The scepter shall not depart from Judah, nor a lawgiver from between his feet, until Shiloh come: and unto him shall the gathering of the people be."

In Genesis 49:28 we read, "All these are the twelve tribes [sceptres] of Israel." The traditional division of Israel into the twelve tribes or sceptres are Reuben, Simeon, (Levi), Judah, Issachar, Zebulum, Benjamin, Dan, Naphtali, Gad, Asher, Ephraim, and Manasseh. Biblical tradition holds that the Twelve Tribes of Israel are descended from the sons and grandsons of Jacob (Gen. 29-30, 35:16-18, 48:5-6). The tribes are collectively called Israel because of their origin in the patriarch Jacob-Israel. They speak a common language or dialect.[1] Jacob and his family went into Egypt as "seventy souls" (Ex. 1:1-15), and then they became the "Israelite people" (Ex. 1:9) (see Appendix C).

At Mount Sinai, the nation received its laws and regulations (Ex. 19:24). After wandering in the desert for forty years under the leadership of Moses, the twelve tribes of Israel penetrated the land of Canaan with Joshua in command. The might of the twelve tribes was more than sufficient to conquer the land. During this time of organization, there was no pattern of leadership among the tribes, except for judges sent to them by God in time of need.[2] Because of the lack of an organized plan of attack and military pressure, the Israelites were compelled to turn to Samuel with the request that he establish a monarchy (see Appendixes D and E).

Saul was crowned to rule over all the tribes of Israel (1 Sam. 11:15). Upon Saul's death, David was chosen to rule from Jerusalem all the tribes of Israel (2 Sam. 5:3). Upon David's death, he was succeeded by his son, Solomon. After the death of Solomon, the tribes split again along political and territorial lines, with Judah and Benjamin in the south loyal to the Davidic house, and the rest of the tribes in the north ruled by a succession of dynasties.[3] Solomon's son, Rehoboam, indicated to the distressed nation that he would be even harder on the people than his father had been.[4] In Rehoboam's fifth year, 918 (1 Kings 14:25), he forsook the law of the Lord and punishment came upon him.[5] For this reason, ten tribes, under the leadership of Jeroboam, separated from the tribes of Judah and Benjamin. Following this division, it was common to use the name "Israel" in referring to the ten northern tribes, and to use the name "Judah" in referring to the two southern tribes (see Appendix F).

In 722 B.C., God allowed the kingdom of Assyria to take the northern ten tribes captive under Shalmaneser, and then under Sargon because of their disobedience and idol worship (2 Kings 17:24) (see Appendix G).

God also allowed the Southern Kingdom to be taken captive because of its refusal to put Jehovah God first in their lives. The Babylonians, under the leadership of Nebuchadnezzar, captured the tribes of Judah and Benjamin. The Babylonians made their first attack on Jerusalem in 605 B.C., and their second attack in 597 B.C. Finally, in 586 B.C., the temple was destroyed by the Babylonians (2 Kings 24:10-16, 25:1-17; 2 Chron. 36:15-21). For seventy years, the Southern Kingdom was in captivity in Babylon (see Appendix H).

TEN LOST TRIBES THEORY

Various theories, one more farfetched than the other, have been mentioned, on unsubstantial evidence, to identify different peoples with the ten lost tribes. There is hardly a people, from the Japanese to the British, and from the Red Indians to the Afghans, who have not been suggested. Among them, Africa, Media, China, Persia, Kudistan, Caucasia, the United States and Great Britain.

Aaron Levi de Montezinos

Special notice is attached to the fantastic traveler's tale by Aaron Levi de Montezinos. On his return to Amsterdam from South Africa in 1644, he told a remarkable story of having found Indians beyond the mountain passes of the Cordilleras who greeted him by reciting the Shema in Hebrew[6]: (שְׁמַע יִשְׂרָאֵל יְהוָה אֱלֹהֵינוּ יְהוָה אֶחָד׃   ) sh' mah yeesrah-el. Ah-doh nye elo-hey-noo ah-doh-nye echod.

Among those to whom Montezinos gave his affidavit was Manasseh Ben Israel, then Rabbi of Amsterdam, who informed Montezinos, through an interpreter, that there were Israelites descended from the tribe of Reuben, and that the tribe of Joseph dwelt in the midst of the sea. He substantiated their claims by tracing Jewish customs among other inhabitants of Central and South America.[7] Manasseh Ben Israel fully accepted the story and to it devoted his *Hope of Israel* (1650-1652), which he dedicated to the English

Parliament. In section 37, we read the following words:

> *1. That the West Indies were anciently inhabited*
> *by a part of the ten Tribes, which passed thither*
> *out of Tartary, by the Streight of Anian. 2. That*
> *the Tribes are not in any one place, but in many;*
> *because the Prophets have fore-told their return*
> *shall be into their Country, out of divers places:*
> *Isaiah especially saith it shall be out of eight. 3.*
> *That they did not return to the Second Temple. 4.*
> *That at this day they keep the Jewish Religion. 5.*
> *That the prophecies concerning the return to*
> *their Country, are of necessity to be fulfilled. 6.*
> *That from all coasts of the World they shall meet*
> *in those two places, sc. Assyria and Egypt; God*
> *preparing an easier, pleasant way, and*
> *abounding with all things, as Isaiah saith.*
> *Chapter 49, and from thence they shall flie to*
> *Jerusalem, as birds to their nests. 7. That their*
> *Kingdom shall be no more divided; but the*
> *twelve Tribes shall be joined together under one*
> *Prince, that is under the Messiah, the Son of*
> *David, and that they shall never be driven out of*
> *their land.*[8]

Eldad ha Dani—David Ruveni

Throughout the Middle Ages and until comparatively recent times, there were claims of the existence of the ten lost tribes. There were attempts by travelers and explorers, both Jews and non-Jews, and by many naive scholars, to discover the ten lost tribes or to identify different people with them. In the ninth century, Eldad ha Dani claimed to be a descendant of the tribe of Dan and noted that the tribes of Dan, Naphtali and Asher were still living in South Arabia and Ethiopia. David Ruveni, a pseudo-messiah who appeared at Venice about

1524, claimed to be a lineal descendant out of the tribe of Reuben and formed an independent kingdom in the Kaibar District of Arabia.[9]

Abyssinia

Other claims have also been advanced at various times that the Falashas of Abyssinia, the Jews of Media and the North American Indians are early descendants of the lost ten tribes. The Karites of Russia also claim to be descendants, and on one occasion declared that they had settled in Crimea shortly after the time of Shalamaneser in the seventh century B.C. Attempts were also made to prove that the Scythians of old and the Japanese are descendants of the lost ten tribes.

Armenians

The late Dr. Chaim Sheba of the Human Genetics Department of the Sheba Medical Center, Tel-Aviv University at Tel-Hashomer, declared the Armenians also could qualify for the ten lost tribes. There seemed to be a similarity between the Armenians and Jews in mental talents, aptitude for chess and business, customs and traditions, facial and body resemblance.[10]

Nestorians

In 1835, Asahel Grant, an American physician, was appointed by the American Board of Foreign Missions to pursue his calling among the Nestorians of Mesopotamia. He found among these people a tradition that they were the descendants of the Lost Ten Tribes confirmed by: (1) they were "beyond the Euphrates" where Josephus had located the Ten Tribes; (2) their language is a branch of the Aramaic; (3) they still offer sacrifices and first fruits like the ancient Israelites; (4) they prepare for the Sabbath on Friday evening, and (5) they have Jewish names and Jewish features. It was also learned that these Nestorians observed the rite of circumcision, offered sacrifices, including that of the Paschal lamb on the twenty-fourth of Nisan (April), and also abstained from forbidden food.[11]

Karites

The Karites of Russia, with their beginning in Bagdad about A.D. 765, come to the forefront as Lost Israel. To avoid persecution, they attempted to prove guiltless of the crucifixion of Jesus, because they were descended from the lost Ten Tribes and were settled in the Crimea since the time of Shalamaneser.[12]

Hindus

Attempts have been made to prove that the Hindus, including all the Buddhists, are descendants of the Scythians, who were the Lost Ten Tribes.[13]

China

Near the Tibetan border, high in the mountains of Szechwan Province of China, dwells a race of worshippers who have called themselves Los Israel. In 1915, a missionary named Torrance identified these people on the basis of the following identifications: (1) monotheism, (2) flatroofed houses, (3) marriage of a widow to the brother of her deceased husband, (4) sacrifice of a "lamb," and (5) certain similarities in words.[14]

The Karens of Burma

The Karens, numbering over a million living in Eastern and Southern Burma, are of a racial nature that seems very different to the Burmese in general. The following points which identify them with Lost Israel are: (1) Jewish appearance, (2) the name used for God ("Yahweh"), and (3) the use of bones of fowls for divination purposes.[15]

Japanese Sect. the Shindai

The Shindai, or holy class of Japan, have been called Lost Israel in a book by N. McLeod, *Epitome of the Ancient History of Japan*. These people were seen as descendants of the Samaritans who were deported with similar characteristics.

1. The first king known in Japan was Osee, 730 B.C., and the last king was Hosea, who died in 722 B.C.

2. The Shinto Temple has two divisions; holy place and a most holy place.

3. Their priests wear a linen dress, bonnet and breeches like the Jewish priest of old.

4. Ancient worship of the Shindai was similar to the patriarchal Israelite worship.

5. Ancient temple instruments are used.

6. The Shindai have "Jewish appearances.[16]

SOURCE OF THE TERM LOST TEN TRIBES

The term "Lost Ten Tribes" does not appear in the Bible. However, it does appear in the mythical and apocryphal book of 2 Esdras. But, we must be careful not to connect the scribe Ezra with 2 Esdras. There is absolutely no connection between these two names in the first century A.D. (2 Esdras 11:1, 12:51). 2 Esdras is a collection of "apocalyptic" visions and does not claim to be a historical narrative. For example:

> *And whereas thou sawest that he gathered another peaceable multitude unto him; those are the ten tribes, which were carried away prisoners out of their own land in the time of Osea the king, whom Salmanasar the king of Assyria led away captive, and he carried them over the waters, and so came they into another land. But they took counsel among themselves, that they would leave the multitude of the heathen, and go forth into a further country,*

> *where never man dwelt, that they might there*
> *keep their statutes, which they never kept in*
> *their own land. And they entered into Euphrates*
> *by the narrow passages of the river. For the*
> *most High then shewed signs for them, and held*
> *still the flood, till they were passed over. For*
> *through that country there was a great way to*
> *go, namely, of a year and a half: and the same*
> *region is called Arsareth.*[17]

Significant of the mythical nature and the confusion as to the whereabouts of the ten lost tribes, Josephus places them "beyond the Euphrates" in the first century A.D., and Esdras has them gone from the Euphrates into "another land." It is very difficult to follow this kind of thinking, because in one place we read that Josephus states that the ten tribes were taken out of Samaria (Antiq. X.IX.7), and at another time were deported from "Judea" (Antiq. IX.XIV.1).

THE ORIGIN OF BRITISH-ISRAELISM

British-Israelism is the theory that the Anglo-Saxons are the physical descendants of the Israelites and that Great Britain, with her daughter, America, has inherited all the covenant blessings given to Abraham.[18]

Very briefly, the Anglo-Israel position is that the Anglo-Saxon peoples, especially Great Britain and the United States, are descended from the tribes of Israel of the Northern Kingdom, and therefore inherit the promises and responsibilities addressed in the Scriptures to Israel. Basically, the Anglo-Saxon nations are the continuation of the nation Israel, the inheritors of her Charters, the possessors of her guarantees and immunities from destruction.[19]

Darms states that British-Israelism can be traced back to a Protestant apologist, Dr. Abadie of Amsterdam, who, in 1723, is quoted as stating, "Unless the ten tribes have flown into the air or have been plunged into the center of the earth, they must be sought for in the south and west, and in the British Isles."[20]

It is quite generally agreed among scholars that Anglo-Saxons originated in the imagination of a very eccentric Briton named Richard Brothers, who bestowed upon himself the title of "Nephew of the Almighty." In 1794 he wrote a book entitled *Revealed Knowledge*, in which he stated that he was a descendant of David and that on November 19, 1795, he would be revealed as the "Prince of the Hebrews." Somehow this did not materialize, and so he produced another book entitled *Correct Account of the Invasion of England by the Saxons, Showing the English Nation to be Descendants of the Lost Ten Tribes*. This volume contains the basic teachings held by Anglo-Saxons to this day. Brothers wrote fifteen books, most arguing for an Israelite ancestry for the English.[21]

Two other men who followed in Brothers' footsteps were John Wilson of England, who published lectures on "Our Israelish Origin," and Edward Hine, who published his book, *Forty-Seven Identifications of the British Nation with Lost Israel*, in London in 1871, and permeated the sect through two magazines, *The Nations Leader* and *Life from the Dead*. Over a quarter million copies of this book were sold and by 1880, Anglo-Israelism had actually crossed the ocean to the "American Cousins."[22]

MODERN PROPONENTS OF BRITISH-ISRAELISM

Today, there are many groups and individuals promoting British-Israelism.

In 1920, Howard B. Rand, manager of a construction company in Haverhill, Massachusetts, began to preach the kingdom message to a small group of Anglo-Israelites and later put out an American Anglo-Israelite publication, first entitled *The Bulletin*, then the *Message of the Covenant*, but now known as *Destiny*, an attractive journal.[23]

A number of years ago, Boake Carter, a well known British-American radio commentator, was persuaded to embrace Anglo-Israelism and to give public testimony to his "conversion experience."[24]

One of the outstanding churches of the Anglo-Israelites is Bethel
Temple in Spokane, Washington, of whom Alexander Schiffner, publisher
of *Prophetic Herald News*, is the pastor (A. M. Greene and Hugh G. Krum
in Portland, in California, Wesley Swift of the Great Pyramid Club, and the
Anglo-Saxon Christian Congregation). In Atascadero, California, there is
a strong work going on under the leadership of William Kullgren, who
publishes *Beacon Light Herald*. Joe Jeffers, who years ago filled the Los
Angeles papers with scandal and finally landed in federal prison, is now in
Sarasota, Florida, with his "Kingdom of Yahweh." At St. Petersburgh,
Florida, we find Kingdom Bible Seminary headed by C. Lewis Fowler.
There is also a Forsythe of Tennessee; Royall of South Carolina; Otis B.
Read, Jr.; pastor of the Open Bible Church in Baltimore; James A. Lovell of
Ft. Worth, who publishes *Kingdom Digest*; Marilyn Allen of Salt Lake; *The
New World Coming* on Dayton, Ohio; Robert B. Record of Chicago; and, of
course, Gerald L. K. Smith, who assists them with his support.[25]

Herbert W. Armstrong

One of the foremost proponents of British-Israelism is Herbert W.
Armstrong and his World Wide Church of God, with headquarters in
Pasadena, California. Much of his teaching is through the media of the *Plain
Truth Magazine*, the *World Tomorrow Broadcast*, and his book, *The United
States and British Commonwealth in Prophecy*. He claims to have 125,000
co-workers of which a number meet regularly in meetings conducted by his
ministers. He has established three colleges; located at Pasadena, California;
Big Sandy, Texas; and at Bricket Wood, England. These schools serve
approximately 1,400 students.

Armstrong's words best sum up his evaluation of his work: "Today
it is a truly great worldwide operation serving 150 million people on all
continents."[26]

In no uncertain terms Armstrong claims that the identification of the
United States and Great Britain in prophecy is the long-lost "key" to the
understanding of the Bible. Armstrongism and Anglo-Israelism is that
which states:

> *The basic premise of the Anglo-Israelites theory
> is that ten lost tribes were lost (Israelites) when
> the Jews were captured by the Assyrians under
> King Sargon and that these so called "lost"
> tribes are in reality, the Saxae, or Scythians,
> who surged westward through Northern Europe
> and eventually became the ancestors of the
> Saxons, who later invaded England. The theory
> maintains that the Anglo-Saxons are the "lost"
> tribes of Israel, and are substituted in Anglo-
> Israel interpretation and exegesis, for the Israel
> of the Bible.*[27]

To further elucidate Armstrong's position regarding the ten lost
tribes, he states:

> *We shall see that these descendants of Joseph,
> possessing these Birthright Promises—to
> become numerous, to colonize, thus spreading
> to the "north and the south, and east and west,"
> until they encircle the globe, to possess the
> "gates" of enemy nations—never returned to
> Jerusalem from Assyria, where they were driven
> with the Ten Tribes after 721 B.C., and were
> never again mixed with the Jews from that time!
> Here are promises and prophecies which never
> have been fulfilled by the Jews, by the Church,
> or other fanciful counterparts of modern
> Israel.*[28]

Armstrong becomes much more definitive when he states:

> *So finally, today, as in Jeremiah's day, the
> House of Israel is in the Isles, which are "in the*

*sea." The Chief of the nations, Northwest of
Jerusalem! A coast-dwelling, and therefore sea-
dominated people.*

*Certainly there can be no mistaking that identity!
Take a map of Europe, lay a line due Northwest
of Jerusalem across the continent of Europe,
until you come to the sea, and then to the islands
in the sea!*

*This line takes you direct to the British Isles!
Of proof that our white, English speaking peoples
today—British and America—are actually and
truly the Birthright tribes of Ephraim and
Manassah of the "lost" House of Israel.*[29]

An absolute essential of Armstrong and British-Israelism is obviously
a Lost Israel. By "lost," Armstrong does not mean merely politically
defunct; he means nationally absent. The system requires more than just the
lostness of the political entity called Israel, but requires the relocation of the
people—all of them. Armstrong explains:

*History does record their captivity by Assyria,
721 through 718 B.C. They were removed from
their cities, towns and farms in their northern
part of Palestine, taken as slaves to Assyria, on
the southern shores of the Caspian Sea.*

*But by 604 to 585 B.C., when the southern
Kingdom of Judah was taken captive by
Nebuchadnezzar of Babylon, the Assyrians had
migrated northwest—and the Ten Tribed
Israelites with them!*

Utterly Lost

They were utterly gone!

They were lost from view!

How far northwest they proceeded, or where they finally settled, comes to a blank page in history.[30]

He also asserts, "The House of Israel did NOT return to Palestine with the Jews in the days of Ezra and Nehemiah, as some erroneously believe."[31]

SUMMARY

This chapter, entitled "The Historical Setting," has set the stage for this dissertation. The pages contain the institution of the Twelve Tribe concept, their movements, monarchy, division and their captivities.

Continuing material is presented on the Lost Ten Tribe theory and the source of this theory. Where did this theory first originate?

Finally, we are introduced to the British-Israelism movement with questions answered like this: What is British-Israelism? Who originated this movement? Who are the leading modern proponents of this movement today? Who publishes their material?

This chapter has set the stage for what is to follow in this paper.

ENDNOTES

[1]   Emil G. Hirsch, "The Twelve Tribes," *Jewish Encyclopedia*, Vol. XII (New York: Funk & Wagnalls, 1916), pp. 254-255.

[2]   H. Fr., "Tribes, the Twelve," *Encyclopedia Judaica*, Vol. XV, SUR-UN, E.J. (Jerusalem: Keter, 1972), p. 1381.

[3]   A. B. MacLean, "Rehoboam," *Interpreter's Bible Dictionary* (New York: Abingdon Press, 1962), p. 29.

[4]   Thomas F. McDaniel, "National Consequences of Leaders' Choices," *Baptist Leader*, July 1, 1979, p. 19.

[5]   MacLean, p. 30.

[6]   Louis Isaac Rabinowitz, "Ten Lost Tribes," *Encyclopedia Judaica*, Vol. XV (Jerusalem: Keter, 1971), p. 1006.

[7]   Joseph Jacobs, "Lost Ten Tribes," *Jewish Encyclopedia*, Vol. XII (New York: Funk & Wagnalls, 1916), p. 250.

[8]   Rabinowitz, p. 1006.

[9]   Rabinowitz, p. 1005.

[10]   Morris Epstein and Allen Howard Godbey, *The Lost Tribes a Myth* (New York: KTAU, 1930), Prolegomenon, pp. 25-26.

[11]   Jacobs, p. 249.

[12]   Jacobs, p. 249.

[13]   Jacobs, p. 249.
[14]   Roger R. Chambers, *The Plain Truth About Armstrongism* (Grand Rapids: Baker, 1972) , p. 32.

[15]   Chambers, p. 33.

[16]   Chambers, p. 33.

[17]   2 Esdras 13:39-45.

[18]   R. P. Nettelhorst, "British-Israelism: A Mirage," *Biblical Research Monthly* (April-May, 1979), p. 21.

[19]   Roy L. Aldrich, *Anglo-Israelism Refuted* (Detroit: Central, 1935), p. 2.

[20]   Anton Darms, *Comprehensive Treatise* (New York: Our Hope, [n.d.], p. 15.

21   Lawrence Duff Forbes, *The Baleful Bubble of "British Israelism"* (Australia: The Biblical Research Society, 1961), p. 11.

22   Edward Hine, *Israel with the Anglo-Celto-Saxons* (New York: Maranatha, [n.d.]), pp. 15, 44-45.

23   Louis T. Talbot, *What's Wrong with Anglo-Israelism?* (Findlay: Dunham, 1956), pp. 5-6.

24   Talbot, p. 6.

25   Talbot, p. 7.

26   Herbert W. Armstrong, "The World Wide Church," *The Plain Truth (February, 1973), pp. 18-19.*

27   Walter Martin, *The Kingdom of the Cults* (Grand Rapids: Zondervan, 1966), p. 295.

28   Martin, p. 295.

29   Martin. p. 115.

30   Martin, p. 152.

31   Martin, p. 89.

CHAPTER 3

THE CLAIMS OF BRITISH ISRAELISM

INTRODUCTION

One who studies this subject in detail will notice that the proponents of British-Israelism make a number of claims and offer a substantial array of proof. The foundation of their beliefs is that the ten tribes of Israel were removed from the land in the Assyrian captivity of 721 B.C., and the people of England and the United States are those lost ten tribes and are heirs of the promises which God made in His covenant with Abraham.

A great number of Biblical passages, ancient texts, theological, geographical, genealogical, physiological, ethnological, historical arguments are offered as proof. Let us examine some of these claims:

The Scepter and Birthright Claims

Anglo-Israelism maintains that the scepter promised to the tribe of Judah refers to the spiritual blessing which came to the world through Jesus Christ. However, the promise of material blessing of prosperity and greatness belongs to the tribes of Ephraim and Manasseh, the sons of Joseph to whom the birthright was given. Ephraim then is regarded as Great Britain and Manasseh is the United States.

This birthright is taken as a promise that the Anglo-Saxon people will achieve world supremacy.

Heath states that the birthright was given unto the sons of Joseph, i.e., Ephraim and Manasseh. Manasseh was to grow into a great people, but Ephraim was to become a multitude of nations (Gen. 48:19). The prophecy finds its fulfillment in these two peoples as in no other.[1]

Allen says:

> *Jacob with his left hand still on Manasseh's head and his right hand on Ephraim's head, continues to prophesy. Manasseh shall be great, but truly his younger brother shall be greater and his seed shall become a multitude of nations.*[2]

At this point we need to clear our minds pertaining to "birthright." Esau, the son of Isaac, was not only in the line of succession, but being the older son, came into possession of the birthright. He sold his birthright to his brother, Jacob, who thus became its possessor. Therefore, Jacob must become the father of that promised multitude of people which is contained in the birthright, i.e., the covenant promise to Abraham.[3]

When God repeated the covenant to Abraham, He added to it by promising the patriarch he would be "a father of many nations" (Gen. 17:4), and further declared, "I will make thee exceedingly fruitful and I will make nations of thee, and kings shall come out of thee" (Gen. 17:6).

This passage states that the seed of Abraham was to spread in all directions. British-Israelism states that the promises to Abraham were twofold:

1. These were kingly spiritual promises. These promises consisted of the royal line and the promised Messiah. These are called the "sceptre" promises which went to Judah (Gen. 49:10). These promises which culminated in Christ are acquired by grace.

2. These were material and national promises which are called the "*birthright*" promises. Birthright has to do with race, not grace, according

to Armstrong. It is acquired simply by being born. It is important to note that the right of the first born was never given to Judah (the Jews). It was given to Joseph (1 Chron. 5:2). Therefore, according to British-Israelism's position, Judah was to receive none of the material promises. Joseph, who became the United States and Britain, received them all.[4]

The Coronation Stone

The Coronation Stone of England, the Stone of Scone, has been known for years and years as "Jacob's Stone,"[5] the stone that Jacob used as a pillow when he fled from his brother, Esau. According to British-Israelism, the stone is kept because the kings and queens of Great Britain are the seed-royal to the house of David. Its history is historical, giving us another of the very many historical proofs we possess in support of our identity. It was taken to Ireland by Jeremiah and Baruch at the time that they took Teplin there, and so planted the kingdom of David. It was called the veritable "stone pillar" whereat the kings of Israel were crowned (2 Kings 11:14). The shout, "God save the King!" that rises to heaven at the coronation is the literal cry of ancient Israel (2 Kings 11:12).[6]

> *The most conspicuous object in the Abbey of Westminster at the coronation service is the throne—standing on a raised platform of five steps in the transept, between the choir and sanctuary. This is King Edward's chair, or the coronation Chair; this famous chair was made in 1300 by order of Edward I, and beneath the seat of which is fixed the Lia-Fail, or Stone of Destiny, believed by many to be the actual stone on which Jacob rested his head at Bethel, consecrating it with oil as "God's house" the morning after his dream of the ladder ascending to heaven.*

The keynote all through the coronation service seems to say, "we are the Israel of God." If we are not the Israel of God, why all these allusions to that effect. This kingdom and empire of Britain is surely God's kingdom, or else where is it.[7]

One of the most splendidly moving events of this century was the coronation of Queen Elizabeth II in London in 1953. She was seated in the coronation chair which contains the legendary "Pillar of Jacob" upon which Israel's patriarch laid his head when he had his symbolically meaningful dream.

Queen Elizabeth was crowned upon "Lia-Phail" which, according to the tradition, had been carried to London from Jerusalem by way of long term resting places; the hill of Tara in Ireland and Iona and Scone in Scotland. The coronation was also a high point in the evolvement of God's servant people, emerging out of their period of punishment, towards the fruition of His blessings. This same stone was prominent at the coronations of King David, and King Solomon, and became the acknowledged throne seat lately occupied by Queen Elizabeth II, full heir to the House of David.[8]

Identification number twenty-six in Ed Hines' book, The British Nation Identified with Lost Israel, states that it is impossible to believe that Jacob's stone is lost. Wherever Israel may be at the present time, they must have the stone in their possession.

The identity of this stone is important. It is further stated that England has a stone which, long before our identity with Israel was thought of and known as "Jacob's Stone." This stone is an object of interest to thousands of tourists who visit Westminster Abbey, as seen under the Seat of the Coronation Chair, the Chief Seat of the Empire and used in coronation services. It was taken to Ireland by Jeremiah and Baruch. It was received into Ireland under the name of "Lia-Phail," meaning a "precious stone," or "The Stone Wonderful." Tephi herself, who became the Queen of Eochaid, was crowned upon it and so were all the other monarchs.[9]

The Throne of David

Proponents of British-Israelism claim that no rightful king of David's line has ruled in Jerusalem since the captivity of Judah. These followers insist that unless descendants of David have ruled in unbroken succession somewhere, God's promise has failed. Therefore, these proponents of British-Israelism teach that the throne of Britain is the continuation of David's royal lineage[10] (see Appendix A).

It is the British-Israelite's view to look at the Davidic Covenant in order to prove that the throne of David must be occupied by a physical personage at all times. God tells David concerning Solomon, "He shall build a house for my name, and I will establish the throne of his kingdom forever" (2 Sam. 7:13).

Armstrong's assertion pertaining to this verse of Scripture is as follows:

> *"He," God continued, "shall build an house for my name, - and it was Solomon who did build the Temple and I will establish the throne of his kingdom Forever."*
>
> *Not only was that throne established forever, it was to exist continuously forever, through ALL GENERATIONS.[11]*

However, this is not all. Armstrong proceeds to quote Scripture: "I have made a covenant with my chosen. I have sworn unto David my servant: Thy seed will I establish forever, and build up thy throne to all generations" (Ps. 89:3-4).

"It was established to all generations, continuously, perpetually, forever! All generations must include those from Zedekiah to the birth of Christ."[12]

Since the house of Judah and the house of Israel are two distinct entities, since the lost ten tribes have found residence in the British Isles, then the throne of England is the perpetuity of the Davidic throne.

The reason for transplanting the Davidic throne to the British Isles is found in the person of the weeping prophet Jeremiah. Listen to what Armstrong says:

> *In view of the linking together of Biblical history, prophecy and Jewish history, can anyone deny that this Hebrew princess was the daughter of King Zedekiah of Judah, and therefore heir to the throne of David? That the aged patriarch was in fact Jeremiah, and his companion Jeremiah's scribe, or secretary, Baruch? And that King Heremon was a descendant of Zarah, heir married to the daughter of Pharez, healing the ancient breach? That when the throne of David was first overturned by Jeremiah, it was replanted in Ireland, later overturned a second time and replanted in Scotland, overturned a third time and planted in London.[13]*

Dr. Clem Daines wrote in his book, *When Jesus Lived in Britain*, the following about the Throne of David:

> *When God appointed David's throne to reign over the house of Israel, he covenanted with King David that his throne would endure forever; as also his house and the kingdom of Israel, over which it was to rule, In other words, there is a throne, there is a house, and there is a people - these things which are to remain and we must find that throne, that people and that house. It is the throne of Westminster, it is the Commonwealth of British Nations.[14]*

Rev. Albon Heath uses the following Scripture (Ps. 39:35-36), to support his claim pertaining to the Throne of David: "Once have I sworn by my holiness that I will not lie unto David. His seed shall endure forever, and his throne as the sun before me."

God made this far-reaching promise, and we believe that God has so fulfilled His promise that there has always been a descendant to occupy the throne. It follows then that this throne must be in existence today and that a descendant occupies that throne or God has lied.

British-Israelism believes the covenants. In Genesis 12:1-3, God made a definite pronouncement which later He confirmed and amplified on oath (Gen. 22:16-18). Israel was to be not only a nation, but a holy nation. The author goes on to say that the word "holy" is the modern form of the Anglo-Saxon word "halig," which means whole or perfect in the sense of all parts functioning in harmony.[15]

Albon Heath, in his book, *The Faith of a British-Israelite,* states:

> *We believe God made this promise, and there has never been lacking a descendant of David to occupy the enduring throne, or God has lied. I have examined briefly the history of every known kingdom in the world in an endeavor to find a throne that met the requirements of this covenant. There is only one such throne in the world, but there is one. It is the throne of Britain.*[16]

> *Remembering that God said the throne of David should be established forever, that it should always be occupied by a descendant of David, and that ultimately our Lord should sit on that throne and reign over the house of Jacob forever. British-Israelites believe that that throne is in existence still, and that its occupant must be a literal descendant of David. The British throne, and King George VI, meet the requirements.*

> *British-Israelites call upon king and people to*
> *acknowledge their identity. The eyes of the world*
> *are turned particularly to the Empire. As the*
> *London Times has said, "The leadership has*
> *fallen to Britain."[17]*

It is impossible to conceal such a racial entity in such a world as ours. It can be identified by the divinely appointed racial and functional marks, and those marks are borne by the British (Covenant) and allied peoples of today. We affirm that the manifold expressions in the Book of Common Prayer which connect the British people with "our forefather Abraham" are not accidental, nor chosen for mere euphony. They express a rare consciousness embedded in the hearts of the people.[18]

Claim of Geography

Church of the Covenant, Pasadena, has this to say in their pamphlet, *The Anglo*-Saxon Celtic Israel Belief:

> *Diligent research into the Bible and historical*
> *records has disclosed the fact that the Anglo-*
> *Saxon Celtic peoples are the lineal descendants*
> *of the House of Israel. Supporting proof is found*
> *in the records of heraldry, the findings of*
> *archaeology and in a study of ethnology and*
> *theology. When the people of the next kingdom*
> *went into Assyrian Captivity, they did not remain*
> *there. They moved westward into the wilderness*
> *across Asia Minor, then into Europe and*
> *eventually into the British Isles.[19]*

In the periodical, New Vision, we read:

> *That we—the English speaking nations with our*

kinfolk in the countries of the North Sea fringe,
embody the birth of the present day descendants
of God's ancient people of Israel. As privileged
servants, He has commissioned us to form the
core of His kingdom on earth.

We assert, therefore, that our associated peoples
are none other than God's promised Company
of Nations—the Commonwealth of Israel—which
the Scriptures declare will be the nucleus of His
earthly Kingdom.

We are able to adduce secular evidence to prove
that the forebears of our kindred peoples
originated in Bible lands. [20]

According to Worth Smith, the British-Israelism writer, the ten tribes remained captive in Assyria less than one hundred years. Becoming unmanageable they moved out of Assyria in 661 B.C., and headed north toward southeastern Europe. Originally they called themselves "the "Sons of Isaac," and ultimately became the Saxons who later invaded England. [21]

Herbert W. Armstrong, the leader of the Cultic Worldwide Church of God, claims that there are many verses in the Bible which support Worth Smith's findings that Israel would move north to occupy a new promised land. According to Armstrong, Amos 9:8-9 indicates Israel will be sifted among the nations. Hosea 3:4 predicts that Israel will abide many days without a king, and 2 Samuel 7:10 and 1 Chronicles 17:9 foretell that Israel will dwell in a permanent place of her own.

Armstrong argues the following:

Notice carefully how all these prophecies fit
together! After being removed from the
Holyland, after being sifted among all nations,
abiding many days without a king, losing their

identity, they are to be planted in a far away,
strange land now to become their own. And they
are to move no more![22]

Armstrong then continues to argue that the strange far away land is
England. Proof that British-Israelism is the Ten Lost Tribes is also offered
by Scripture, for in Genesis 28:14 we read:

And thy seed shalt be as the desert of the earth,
and then shalt spread abroad to the west, and to
the east, and to the north and to the south: And
in these and thy seed shall all the families of the
earth be blessed. (Gen. 28:14)

Howard Rand, in his book, *The Covenant People,* is basically
concerned with the identity of the House of Israel and its westward drive to
the Appointed Place—the Isles north and west of Palestine. The climax of
this fascinating story is the final arrival of the Manasseh branch of the
people of the House of Israel upon the shores of the North American
continent.[23]

Because of the turmoil going on during the captivity, there was
certainly no inducement for Israel to go back to their own land for two
reasons. First, the Babylonian armies blocked the way. Second, Assyria had
populated the land with other peoples; Arabs, Babylonians, Persians and
people from Susiano. But as I read my Bible and trace their route on the old
map, corroborated by the ancient historians, I arrive at the answer that Israel
did so go out.[24]

Mr. Rand goes on to say, in his book, *The Covenant People,* that if
you will look at a map of Europe and Western Asia, you will find that if you
look straight up the Adriatic to Germany, Holland and Britain from ancient
Israel, you will come to the British Isles of the West[25] (see Appendix J).

British-Israelism makes much out of the fact that God would "plant"
His people in a particular place and that they should not move any more (2
Sam. 7:10), and that this PLACE could not possibly have been Palestine

because they were IN Palestine when this prophecy was made.[26]

To follow up on the word "plant" which Rand talks about, we must turn to pp. 209-210 in Allen's book, *Judah's Sceptre and Joseph's Birthright*. These people who have been taken out of their own land and "planted" in another is by "great waters." In their new home, Israel "grew and became a spreading vine."[27] On p. 227, Allen actually calls these Isles Britain.

The Philological Claim

British-Israelism claims that the Hebrew language is closely related to Keltic and Anglo-Saxon, and that there are many names which clearly prove their identity with Israel. The declared opinion of eminent scholars is that the English language contains the roots of no less than eight hundred Hebrew words.

It is not our purpose to give them here, yet we insert a few by way of illustration:

English	Hebrew	English	Hebrew
Sever	Shaver	Crocus	Cro Cum
Sabbath	Shabbath	Balsam	Ba Sam
Scale	Shakal	Garner	Ga Kan
Kitten	Qui Ton	Garden	Ge DaR
Goat Kid	Gi Di	Hob	BaB
Doe	Tod	Tar	TaR
Gum	Gam	Light	LahT

(This is in reference to Isa. 28:11 and Jesus telling the Israelites that they would speak in a different language. The author claims that they changed their language to English.)[28]

Gladys Taylor states:

> *From our own point of view, it is the sheer*
> *weight of evidence contained in all the ancient*
> *languages of the British Isles that is important*
> *and, combined with the incidence of significant*
> *place names, forms strong proof of our Shemite*
> *and Hebrew ancestry.*[29]

It is important to understand the British-Israelism position when we talk about language to definitely prove that we are of the Hebrew ancestry. British-Israelism would like to present two such claims.

1. The Hebrew word, "beirth" (בְּרִית) or "birth" (בְּרִית) This word occurs more than a hundred times in the Old Testament and is always translated "covenant." "Ish" (אִישׁ) is the Hebrew word for "man," hence, Brithish, or British, literally means "covenant man." Adam Rutherford calls our attention to the fact that the Hebrew word for "ain" (עַיִן) means "land," and that the Hebrew sound "annia" means ships. Thus, it should be concluded to everyone that Brit-ain is the land of the covenant people and Brit-annia ships of the covenant — "rule the waves."[30]

2. The Claim for the Danite character of Denmark points to occasional recurrences of the syllable "dan" in geographical names from the Dandanelly to Danelagh.[31]

As we follow the tribe of Dan and try to prove they settled in Ireland, they point to words like "din," "dun," or "dan," which is a part of the name of a territory, city or river where they passed through or settled. A few names mentioned by British-Israelism are Macedonia, Dardanelles, Danube, Denmark and Dunbar.[32]

3. British-Israelism states that the word "Saxon" is also Hebrew and that it has the meaning, "Isaac's sons." They state that every Saxon is an "Isaac son."[33]

Israel vs Judah Claim

Armstrong claims that the House of Israel is not Jewish.
Jews are Israelites, just as Californians are Americans. But most

Israelites are not Jews, just as most Americans are not Californians. The Jews are the House of Judah only, a part of the Israelites. But when these people are spoken of as nations, rather than collective individuals, the term "Israel" never refers to the Jews. "House of Israel" never means "Jews." The two tribes at Jerusalem under the Davidic king are called, merely, the House of Judah.[34]

According to Herbert W. Armstrong, there is a definite difference between the terms "Israel" and "Jew."

In pinpointing this difference between these two words, Armstrong says:

> *We want to impress here that Israel and Judah*
> *are not two names for the same nation. They*
> *were and still are, and shall be until the Second*
> *Coming of Christ, two separate nations. The*
> *House of Judah always means Jew.*[35]

In Jeremiah 13:11, we have undisputable proofs of the two houses, since the broadest generic terms possible are used. Here it is:

> *For as a girdle cleaveth to the loins of man, so*
> *have I caused to cleave unto me the whole house*
> *of Israel and the whole house of Judah, saith the*
> *Lord; that they might be unto me for a people,*
> *and for a name, and for a praise, and for a*
> *glory; but they would not hear.*

This statement gives us to understand that "the whole house of Israel" are not all of the Lord's people, but that it takes "the whole house of Israel" together with "the whole house of Judah" to make all of his chosen people.

It also proves that there is a people called "the whole house of Israel" of which "the whole house of Judah" is regarded as neither part nor parcel.[36]

Allen goes on to say that the name "Jew" is derived from, or rather is a corruption of, the name of Judah (singular Ju-dah, or Jew-dah; plural, Ju-dahs, or Jew-dahs; possessive, Ju-dah's, or Jew-dah's; contracted, Jew, Jews and Jew's). Hence it is that the names Jew and Jews are applied only to the people who composed the Kingdom of Judah.[37]

Thus, we see that the name of Ephraim is used as a representative name for the northern Kingdom, just as the name of Judah is used for the southern Kingdom, and that the names Israel, Ephraim and Samaria are used as names of the ten-tribed Kingdom in contradistinction to those of the three-tribed Kingdom, which are Judah, Jerusalem and the Jews.[38]

The first time the word Jews is used in the history of the Abrahamic race is at a time when the Jews and Israel were at war with each other. Hence we ask, if the Jews were the besieged and Israel was with the besiegers, how can it be possible that the Jews and Israel are one and the same people?[39]

Edward Hine, in his book, *The British Nation Identified with Lost Israel, says,* "when God, in prophecy, speaks to the House of Israel, He does not refer to the Jews; and when He refers to Judah, it is generally as distinct from Israel."[40] He goes on to say the Jews are "of Israel," therefore purely Israelites, but the people of the Ten Tribes were never Jews.

Jeremiah 3.8 is in complete harmony with the other writers that have been quoted, showing that the Twelve Tribes are to be two distinct peoples till the return of Palestine. For until the end they are spoken of as the "remnant" of the Jews, and the "outcasts" of Israel, who are then to be a "strong nation."[41]

In the beliefs of British-Israelism we find these statements in Sections 1, 2, and 3.

Section 1: Judah and Israel are entirely distinct and separate entities (2 Chron. 11).

Section 2: Israel was to constitute a kingdom, but the Jews were never to be a nation until reunited with Israel. Jews were to remain under the law and Old Testament, whereas Israel was to be a Christian people.

Section 3: Israel had nothing to do with the crucifixion of our Lord.

Consequently, the curse of God rests upon them, whereas, the ten tribes—or British-Israelism—have no blame in this matter. The fact remains that the Romans and the Jews crucified our Lord and the whole world is guilty of His death. All the promises and blessings go to Israel and all the curses are passed on to the Jews.

The Claim That Great Britain is the Ten Lost Tribes of Israel

During the reign of Israel's last king, Hoshea, the House of Israel was conquered and its people driven out of their land—their home—their cities and carried captives to Assyria. And then . . . lost from view![42] 2 Kings 17:18 says, "Therefore the Eternal was very angry with Israel, and removed them out of his sight. There was none left but the tribe of Judah only."

Armstrong quotes Scripture, 1 Kings 17:23, which says, "Carried away out of their own land to Assyria." The conclusion of many Jewish scholars and historians is that the House of Israel did not return with those of the House of Judah. The House of Israel became known as the "Lost Ten Tribes," now known by another name, speaking a different language.[43]

In *The National Message*, June, 1980, one finds these words: "Admiral Sir John Fisher, at the peak of British sea-power, was able to say, 'the only hypothesis to explain why we win in spite of incredible blunders is that we are the lost ten tribes of Israel.'"[44]

Armstrong made the following statement: "If we are not national Israel so called 'lost Ten Tribes'—prosperous Joseph Israel—Birthright Israel—actual inheritors of the Birthright blessings which were to be bestowed beginning 1800 A.D., then Who Else Can Be?"[45]

Edward Hine says, "The identity indicates the worldknown fact, that the British nation has the most powerful army in the world; Israel's was to be the most powerful: Ergo, we must be Israel."[46]

It is important at this juncture to present original source material from one who was the imitator of British-Israelism. From its inception there was no doubt that Great Britain was the Ten Lost Tribes of Israel.

Mr. Hines continues:

> *My objective in coming prominately before the*
> *country is to prove that the British people are*
> *identical with the Lost Tribes, and to do this, I*

> *propose to advance forty-seven clear and
> positive identifications, that shall be supported
> by 500 Scripture proofs.*[47]

Basically, British-Israelism teaches that the House of Israel (ten tribes) lost their identity after they were captured by the Assyrians in the eighth century B.C., and that they drifted westward through northern Europe and became the ancestors of the Saxons, who later invaded England.

> *Tarshish will be a mercantile and maritime
> people— the first to carry back Israel to the
> Holy Land. . . . Putting all together, Ezekiel
> requires us to find in Europe, among the Isles of
> the Gentiles, in these latter times, a mercantile,
> colonising, manufacturing, warlike power such
> as Tyre, a great world's mart, commanding the
> trade of the East and West; but especially the
> trade of the eastern seas. That power, like God's
> confederates, must be now before the world, and
> there is one power that can answer such a
> description—It is England!*[48]

This well known name is also the latter day name of the outcast and lost "House of Joseph," or "Israel," and the Jews have to walk to the House of Israel (Great Britain), to be reinstated in their own land! The prophet has just described the return of the Ten Tribes, who are to be brought to Zion, and of the Gentiles, who are to make Jerusalem their home: if Judah repents she cannot possibly be left out. But Israel is represented as the first to repent, and Judah must go to her in order that they may come *tog*ether back to the Holy Land, divided no longer into Jews and Israelites, but merged into one people.

Hence, from this and other Scriptures, it seems indisputable that the strong and powerful nation who will take back the Jews in her own ships of Tarshish can be no other than "the chief of the nations," the "strong nation," in "the Isles afar off," in the "West," i.e., the "outcast House of Israel" (Isa. 9:12), or the so-called "Lost Ten Tribes," even Great and Greater Britain.

Again, inquire of any man of the world what great maritime nation will probably occupy Palestine, give protection to the Jews, and also (as "the merchants of Tarshish, with all the young lions thereof") have to withstand Russia over the final settlement of the burning "eastern Question?" His answer will give the present name of the lost "House of Israel"—viz., Great Britain.[49]

The "splendid isolation" of Great Britain has become a well known taunt, but it is written of Israel: "Lo, it is a people that shall dwell alone, and shall not be reckoned among the nations" (Num. 23:9). The author claims that Britain is the Power called the "King of the South." Then it concludes, therefore, if Great Britain be the Power called "the King of the South," in these last days, it follows that Great Britain is the House of Israel, in spite of the unjust and frivolous objections that are raised by some against this view.

The great empires that are to be brought face to face over the Eastern Question are fully described in God's Word. Daniel 11:40-45 informs us that at "the time of the end," the "King of the North" is to come up against the "King of the South," that he overflows, passes through and enters into the glorious land. This great Power, the King of the North (the God of Ezek. 38), nearly overwhelms the King of the South.

This has indeed come to pass, and with our fresh advance into the Sudan, it is not very likely that Great Britain will get out of Egypt before the Eastern crisis becomes acute. Besides, as "God" is the same Power as "the King of the North," it is very evident that Great Britain must be the "King of the South," for hardly any student of prophecy doubts whom Gog or Russia comes up against over the final settlement of the Eastern Question.

Again, those who are to suffer under Gog's invasion are undoubtedly God's chosen people, "even My people Israel"—Israel and Judah. So, logically, it clearly follows that if Gog and the King of the North be the same Power, even Russia and her combined hosts, then the "King of the South," and "My People Israel," against whom his northern Power comes up, must also be identical. No one doubts that it is Israel that Gog comes up against, and yet we are laughed at when we say "the King of the South" must also be part of God's people Israel.[50] We maintain that logically no one can get out of this difficulty except by owning that the King of the South is part of God's chosen race. But it cannot be Judah or the Jews.

It is indeed a matter of historical proof if those who do not yet see this truth would only carefully study the literature of this important subject, that the ancestors of the Anglo-Saxon race, who are now dwelling where the House of Israel was prophesied to dwell in "the latter days," and fulfilling the various predictions spoken of that House, while in the lands of their exile, came from the very spot to which Israel was taken after their captivity by the Assyrians, and, therefore, can clearly be proved historically to be descended from the lost Ten Tribes.[51]

Sharon Turner, our own historian, must be relied upon as he quotes from the classic historians, i.e., Homer, Starbo, Herodotus, Pliny and Ptolemy. The extracts of these giants prove that our so-called Saxon ancestors came from the area of the world where Israel became lost. Also, that in the days of Christ our forefathers were actually living in the northwest of Asia on their way to Europe. Also to strengthen our argument we find that in the days of the Apostles, the British race was actually located in Asia Minor.

Christ's command to His disciples was to go to the lost sheep of the House of Israel (Matt. 15:24) and in obedience to this command we see these witnesses going to the precise area where our forefathers were located.[52]

According to Homer, the first appearance of the British Empire in Media was at the exact time of the Assyrian captivity of Israel. Could this be coincidental? Of course not.[53]

Because of Israel's sins, she could not be known by the name "Ammi," or my nation, my people, which Israel means, but this name must be taken from her and therefore should be known as "Lo-ammi," i.e., not my nation (Hosea 1:9), so with her name and ancestry lost, "The British Nation" could only be the other name.[54]

Israel in exile would speak another tongue, but not Hebrew. We maintain, as Britons, that because we have adopted the English language and not the Hebrew tongue, this is proof of our identity.[55]

Israel must have, and be in possession of colonies. We maintain that colonies must now be an institution of Israel's because the prayer that Israel raised when in the isles was heard by God. The prayer is, "The place is too strait for me; give place to me that I may dwell" (Isa. 49:20). In verse 8 of the same chapter, we read, "I will preserve thee and give thee . . . to establish the earth, to cause to inherit the desolate heritages." These "desolate heritages" are colonies.

The fact that the British nation has colonies which were only promised to Israel shows clearly that we must be Israel and therefore are the only nation upon the earth that has succeeded in colonizing.[56]

To close this section as to the claim of British-Israelism that they are the Lost Ten Tribes, this author will quote from M. Thomas Starkes' book, *Confronting Popular Cults.*

> *In 1928, M. H. Gayer of London wrote one of the standard works of the movement, The Heritage of the Anglo-Saxon Race. This book included a chart "proving" that Great Britain and the United States are really the lost tribes of Ephraim and Manasseh.[57]*

The Anglo-Saxon Federation of America, publishers of *Destiny Magazine*, stated that "Israel left Palestine while the Jew remained. The movements of the Israel clans are traced out of the East across Europe, to their new settlement in the Isles of Britain and then on to America."[58]

Race vs Grace

J. H. Allen, in his book, *Judah's Sceptre and Joseph's Birthright,* states that the Covenant nations must come *only* from Abraham and Sarah through their only son, Isaac, whose posterity alone can be called the Children of the Promise,[59] followed by Jacob.

The crucial test before us is that they be Abraham's seed who have descended from Isaac through Jacob. Thus, it is logical that the natural seed

of Abraham are the children of promise, and no one else, even though they
were natural sons of Abraham they are still "the Children of the Flesh" only.
Only to Israelites, the seed of Abraham, Isaac and Jacob, are given the
promises, the covenants, the adoption, the glory, the special service, the
giving of the divine law, and through whom Christ came.

We must again realize that the order is Abraham, Isaac and Jacob, not
Abraham, Ishmael and Esau. Therefore, the racial name is Israel. Thus, each
individual member of the race is an Israelite and belongs to the elect or
chosen people of God.[60]

Allen goes on to say the following:

> When it is race, it is, "Whom I (God) have
> chosen."

> When it is grace, it is, "Whosoever will, may
> come."

> When it is race, it is, - "I have called thee by my
> name, thou art mine."

> When it is grace, "Whosoever believeth." In
> grace it is, "Come."

> In race it is fate, destiny.

> One is a chosen race, and the other a chosen
> way. The choice of race is according to the
> predetermined and predestined purpose of God.
> In race election, it is generation, or born of the
> flesh.

> In the election of grace it is regeneration, or
> born of the spirit.

*In grace it is, "Whosoever offereth praise
glorifieth me; but in race, it is, "This people
have I formed for myself."*[61]

Armstrong makes the following remarks when it comes to race
versus grace: "(1) He takes his chosen—race doctrine and logically holds
for strict segregation of races; (2) That Israel is still the chosen race."[62]

The Sabbath Claim

Listen to what Armstrong has to say pertaining to the Sabbath: "I
have said that God made the Sabbath a separate, eternal, and Perpetual
Covenant, entirely separate and apart from what we term the Old Covenant
made at Mt. Sinai."[63]

Armstrong sees the Sabbath as the independent and eternal covenant
that identifies the people of God.

In Exodus 31 we read to whom the command to observe the Sabbath
was given: "Wherefore the children of Israel shall keep the sabbath, to
observe the sabbath throughout their generations, for a perpetual covenant"
(v. 16). "It is a sign between Me and the children of Israel forever" (v. 17).

The Anglo-Saxon race was and are the only people to observe this
sign. In the past, when foreigners were questioned as to what impressed
them most about English and American customs, they replied, "Your
English Sunday." While all places were wide open in foreign lands, in
Britain and America, the Sabbath was observed.[64]

SUMMARY

The claims presented in this chapter have come from the leading
sources of British-Israelism. There has been no tampering with their books,
writings or quotes.

The presentation has been honest with believers with no ulterior
motives to harm or do any injustice to those who embrace British-Israelism.

ENDNOTES

1   Albon Heath, *The Faith of a British Israelite* (London: Covenant, 1937), p. 63.

2   J. A. Allen, *Judah's Sceptre and Joseph's Birthright* (Merrimac: Destiny, 1917),
p. 46.

3   Allen, pp. 38-40.

4   H. W. Armstrong, *The United States and British Commonwealth in Prophecy*
(Pasadena: Ambassador, 1975), pp. 20-24, 37-39.

5   Edward Hine, *The British Nation With the Lost Ten Tribes* (London: Partridge,
[n.d.]), p. 34.

6   Howard B. Rand, *The Covenant People* (Merrimac: Destiny, 1972), p. 59.

7   J. H. Rambeston, *The Coronation Service* (Bedford, BIWF, [n.d.]), pp. 7-9.

8   J. A. B. Haggart, "Elizabeth--Monarch of Destiny," *Wake Up,* July, 1980, p. 14.

9   Ed Hines, *The British Nation Identified with Lost Israel* (London: S. W. Partridge,
1964), p. 35.

10   Richard W. DeHaan, *British Israelism* (Grand Rapids: DeHaan, 1969), p. 12.

11   Worth Smith, *The House of Glory* (New York: Wise, 1939), p. 28.

12   Armstrong, p. 70.

13   Armstrong, pp. 122-123.

14   Dr. Clem Daines, *When Jesus Lived in Britain* (California: Clem Daines, [n.d.]),
pp. 4-5.

15   Heath, pp. 24, 36.

16   Heath, p. 49 .

17   Heath, p. 49.

18   Heath, p. 83.

19   Church of the Covenant, *The Anglo-Saxon Celtic Israel Belief,* Pasadena, California,
1969.

20   "We Believe," *New Vision,* April-June, 1969, p. 3.

21   Smith, pp. 70-72.

22   Herbert W. Armstrong, *The U.S. and British Commonwealth in Prophecy* (Pasadena: Ambassador, 1972), p. 125.

23   Rand, p. 4.

24   Rand, p. 39.

25   Rand, p. 46.

26   Charles W. Walkem, *British Israelism Myth* (Los Angeles: Church Press, 1948), p. 14.

27   Allen, pp. 209-210.

28   Hine, *British Nation Identified with Lost Israel,* pp. 15-16.

29   Gladys Taylor, *Our Neglected Heritage: Division and Dispersion* (London: Covenant, 1974), p. 39.

30   C. R. Dickey, *One Man's Destiny (Merrimac: Destiny,* 1951), pp. 265-266.

31   Dickey, p. 226.

32   Howard Rand, *Anglo-Saxon Federation of America* (Haverhill: Destiny, 1928). See Appendix B.

33   Dickey.

34   Armstrong, p. 82.

35   Armstrong, p. 84.

36   Allen, p. 65.

37   Allen, p. 66.

38   Allen, p. 69.

39   Allen, p. 74.

40   Hine, *British Nation Identified with Lost Israel,* p. 1.

41   H. Aldersmith, *The Fullness of the Nations* (London: Marshall, 1898), p. 130.

42   Armstrong, p. 37.

43   Armstrong, p. 39.

44   Admiral Sir John Fisher, *The National Message,* 59, No. 1687 (June, 1980), p. 87.

45   Armstrong, p. 24.

[46]   Hine, *British Nation Identified With Lost Israel*, p. 38.

[47]   Hine, *British Nation With Lost Ten Tribes*, p. 43.

[48]   Aldersmith, p. 136.

[49]   Aldersmith, p. 137.

[50]   Aldersmith, p. 139.

[51]   Aldersmith, p. 144.

[52]   Hine, *British Nation Identified with Lost Israel*, p.6.

[53]   Hine, *British Nation Identified with Lost Israel*, p. 7.

[54]   Hine, *British Nation Identified with Lost Israel*, p. 14.

[55]   Hine, *British Nation Identified with Lost Israel*, p. 15.

[56]   Hine, *British Nation Identified with Lost Israel*, pp. 18-19.

[57]   M. Thomas Starkes, *Confronting Popular Cults* (Nashville: Broadman, 1972), p. 45.

[58]   Starkes, p. 45.

[59]   Allen, p. 26.

[60]   Allen, pp. 30-31.

[61]   Allen, p. 32.

[62]   Roy R. Chambers, *The Plain Truth About Armstrongism* (Grand Rapids: Baker, 1972), p. 103.

[63]   Armstrong, p. 161.

[64]   George F. Jarrett, *The Drama of the Lost Disciples* (London: Covenant, 1978), p. 55.

CHAPTER 4

A REFUTATION TO THE CLAIMS OF BRITISH-ISRAELISM

INTRODUCTION

One of the most fantastic, most entertaining and yet most tragic misinterpretations of the Word of God to be imposed on the Christian world is that of British-Israelism or Anglo-Israelism. This far-fetched theory is built around the central theme that the Anglo-Saxon peoples are the lost tribes of Israel. In an attempt to answer the question, "Who and where are the lost ten tribes?" the originators of this sect have included everything; from the throne of David to the Great Pyramid of Egypt; from Jeremiah the prophet to the United States flag; from the coronation stone to the harp "that hung in Tara's hall"!

Because there is no historical and Scriptural basis for the claims that British-Israelism makes, they are forced to turn to legends, traditions, folklore and the Apocryphal writings to obtain sufficient basis for their theory. The Apocryphal writings are wholly unreliable for they do not claim inspiration. The Jews have never accepted them as a part of the Jewish canon even though they are good history. Jesus Christ never quoted from these books, but yet Anglo-Israelites use these writings.

Many of the interpretations of British-Israelism are not only bordering on blasphemy, but are blasphemous to say the least.

The advocates of British-Israelism say, "Anglo-Israelism is now considered the most important religious subject in the world." In contrasting their claims with the Bible and history, The British nation is brought into the picture as a Great nation, but not the gathering place of the Ten Tribes of Israel.[1]

The writer has the highest regard for Great Britain and the Royal family. However, this author must be honest to himself and his readers by saying that too many Christians who really love the Lord have been mislead with the romantic but unscriptural teaching of Anglo-Israelism.

After two years of research, the writer has come to the conclusion that this entire system is a delusion of Satan, a denial of the redemptive work of the Lord Jesus Christ, a presentation of a false Messiah and the lack of honest exegesis of the Word of God.

The following pages of refutation of the claims of British-Israelism are written with no personal animosity toward those who hold the Anglo-Israelism viewpoint, but with the hope of making known the truth concerning a dangerous and unscriptural theory which has been damaging to many of God's people in the twentieth century.

Each of the claims in Chapter 3 will be refuted.

Sceptre and Birthright

How these people who seem to have the key to Biblical interpretation can mishandle Scripture is beyond this author. Many Scripture verses are given by British-Israelism that support their contention that Great Britain is Israel. For example, there are passages in the Bible which promise certain blessings to Israel. British-Israelism claims that Britain has been blessed in the same way, therefore Britain must be Israel. British-Israelism divides "scepter" promises from "birthright" promises as we have seen in Chapter 3, pp. 20-22, with the scepter promises of the Throne of David and Messiah reserved to Judah, while the birthright promises of material blessings are reserved to Joseph. However, a detailed look at Deut. 27-30 is enough to dispel this myth even from a novice of the Scriptures.

Not only is *all* of Israel promised material blessings (28:1-14), but *all* twelve tribes are also promised cursings (28:15-68)—not just Judah. Blessings will not be restored until Israel returns to the promised land, which is the land of Palestine alone (30:1-5; Gen. 15:18-21, 17:7-8; Ezek. 37). Even if Great Britain and the United States were the Israelites, they could not, under any circumstances, have the blessings of God until they were back in the land of Canaan.

This author will now deal with the proponents of British-Israelism in their treatment of two verses of Scripture: "The scepter shall not depart from Judah, nor a law-giver from between his feet, until Shiloh come; and unto him shall the gathering of the people be" (Gen. 49:10); and, "For Judah prevailed above his brethren, and of him came the chief ruler; but the birthright was Joseph's" (1 Chron. 5:2).

There is a definite distinction between these promises. The Anglo-Saxons believe the birthright promise people will achieve world supremacy because material prosperity and greatness belong to the tribes of Ephraim and Manasseh, the sons of Joseph, to whom the birthright was given. This is 1981, which, to this writer, reveals the utter fallacy of their thinking.

The birthright simply granted the double portion of the inheritance, which the eldest son normally received. Reuben, Jacob's oldest son, forfeited his birthright through sin. Because of this, Joseph's two sons, Ephraim and Manasseh, each received a full share along with Joseph's brother. Thus, Joseph, through his two sons, inherited the double portion that normally would have gone to Reuben. Basically, this is all that is involved with the *birthright*.

The "scepter promise" has nothing to do with the birthright. Notice in Gen. 49:10 the word "scepter" (שֵׁבֶט). Shebet is a translation of a Hebrew word, "tribe,"[2] *141* times in the Old Testament, and the expression "nor a lawgiver from between his feet," means that governmental authority and power represented in the chief executive shall continue with the tribe of Judah until the one "whose right it is" comes. Here in these lines is the promise that an unbroken line of rulers will continue in Judah and reach its climax in the coming of the redeemer of the world. The promise is that *all* nations will obey Him.[3]

The late David Baron, outstanding Old Testament scholar, summarizes the consensus of scholars concerning Gen. 49 :10 as reflected in the earliest versions and commentaries of the Hebrew people:

> *With regard to this prophecy, the first thing I want to point out is that all antiquity agrees in interpreting it of a personal Messiah. This is the view of the LXX version; the Targumism of Onkelos, Yonathan, and Jerusalem; the Talmud; the Soliar; the ancient book of "Bershith Rabba"; and among modern Jewish commentators, even of Rashi, who says, "Until Shiloh come, that is King Messiah, whose is the "kingdom."[4]*

The attempt to establish a Scriptural basis for the theory that Ephraim and Manasseh represent Great Britain and the United States is obviously futile and completely without merit. How any honest and intelligent person can believe this is beyond the comprehension of this writer.

Coronation Stone

How British-Israelism can believe that the coronation stone is kept because the leaders of Great Britain are the seed royal to the House of David is beyond any intellectual comprehension. The leading people in England are aware that the story of the stone is only legendary and they keep it as a symbol or for tradition sake.

When one talks about the stone, the stone is none other than the one which is under the coronation throne in Westminster Abbey where kings and queens of England are crowned. Legend comes in again as practically everything that British-Israelism believes. But let us examine this stone. The Coronation Stone is a dull reddish or purplish sand stone (the writer saw this) with a few pebbles embedded in it, and there is complete agreement among geologists that no stone like this ever came from the land of Palestine. Investigation from scientists who have analyzed the stone of Scone have found it to be definitely of Scottish origin.[5]

The writer bought a pictorial history of Westminster Abbey at the Abbey and this is what it had to say under the picture of the Coronation Chair.

> *The ancient Coronation Chair stands in St. Edwards Chapel but is transferred to the centre of the "theatre" for a coronation. Fashioned by Master Walter of Durham in 1300 it was made to the order of Edward I to enclose the Stone of Scone, a block of reddish grey sandstone, which he had captured from the Scots in 1296. According to legend this was the stone upon which Jacob laid his head and dreamed his dream. The Kings of Scotland were placed upon it at their coronations. Since 1296 the Coronation Chair with the stone enclosed has been used for every coronation with the exception of Edward V and Edward VIII who were never crowned.[6]*

Without reservation there is no Bible basis for this outlandish poppycock about the Coronation Stone being Jacob's stone where he laid his head after wrestling with God. Instead, the Bible teaches that Jacob *did not* take the "pillar-stone" with him, but left it for a memorial of God's faithfulness to him. "And this stone, which I have set for a pillar, shall be God's house" (Gen. 28:22). "And Jacob set up a pillar in the place where he talked with him, even a pillar of stone" (Gen. 35:14).

Jacob placed that stone as a memorial long before Israel had become a nation, or had ever gone to Egypt for the captivity. How ridiculous to think that his descendants carried this for four hundred years and then through the wilderness to the promised land and finally on to England.

Howard B. Rand, in his book, *The Covenant People*, makes another Biblical blunder when he states, "the stone was taken to Ireland by Jeremiah, then to the British Isles."[7]

There is no Scriptural evidence that Jeremiah ever went to the British Isles with the stone. Jacob left the stone at Bethel. British-Israelism would do well to do likewise.

As to the evidence of the stone itself, Mr. Marson, who was in the Armstrong camp for ten years, states, "The stone in Westminster Abbey has been analyzed and shown to be a calcareous type of red sandstone of Scottish origin."[8]

For further support is presented a bit of geological evidence from the well-known authority, C. F. Davidson. He states that there is "no authority for the view" that this stone originated in Palestine and that the:

> *whole balance of evidence, thereupon, is in favor of the Stone having been quarried somewhere in the east of Perthshire, or in southern Scotland, probably not far from the ancient seat of the Pictish monarchy at Scone . . . from this study of the Coronation Stone is seen to agree most closely in lithology with sandstones of Lower Old Red Sandstone from Scotland. In other words, it was an ordinary Scotch rock!*[9]

The Throne of David

God's unconditional covenant with David is recorded in 2 Sam. 7:12-16. This promise assured David that his successor would be one of his own sons, that this son would build the temple, and that Yahweh God would never take the kingship of Israel from his family. God, through this Scripture, assured David that his house, his throne and his kingdom, would endure forever and so these promises of God were honored.

British-Israelism insists that unless descendants of David have ruled in *unbroken succession* somewhere, God's promise has failed. Therefore, they teach that the throne of Britain is the continuation of David's royal lineage.

The foundation for British-Israelism's error in this area is their misunderstanding of the Davidic Covenant. They fail to consider some of the Bible verses that have to do with God's promise to David. The conclusion seems to be a literal earthly throne from the time of David to this day, and forever.

God's covenants with Abraham and David were unconditional. This means that the disobedience of men would not be permitted to frustrate God's plan. Willful sin, however, always results in chastening, and when God promised David the perpetuity of his house and throne, He warned that if his descendants were disobedient, they would be disciplined. "I will be his father, and he shall be my son. If he commit iniquity, I will chasten him with the rod of men, and with the stripes of the children of men" (2 Sam. 7:14).

Nowhere in Scripture did God ever tell David that his descendants would rule in unbroken succession. However, He did say a royal seed and kingdom would be established forever. God never said "through all succeeding generations *without* interruption." Let us see what the Psalmist has to say:

> *The Lord hath sworn in truth unto David; he will*
> *not turn from it; of the fruit of thy body will I set*
> *upon thy throne. If thy children will keep my*
> *covenant and my testimony that I shall teach*
> *them, their children shall also sit upon thy throne*
> *forevermore. (Ps. 132:11-12)*

David adds:

> *And he said unto me, Solomon thy son, he shall*
> *build my house and my courts; for I have chosen*
> *him to be my son, and I will be his father.*

> *Moreover I will establish his kingdom forever, if*
> *he be constant and to do my commandments and*
> *my judgments, as at this day. (1 Chron. 28:6-7)*

There is no question that God has established David's throne forever in Christ, the son of David. There was never any doubt in David's mind that the literal establishment of that throne in his early descendants depended upon their obedience to the commandments of God.

It is Armstrong's contention that because of the Davidic covenant, the Davidic throne must always be occupied by a physical personage. It is perhaps in this area where Armstrong demonstrates his greatest ignorance, not only of the Davidic covenant, but also of the Scriptures as a whole. Walvoord correctly asserts:

> *What do the major terms of the covenant mean?*
> *. . . . By the term throne it is clear that no*
> *reference is made to a material throne, but*
> *rather to the dignity and power which was*
> *sovereign and supreme in David as king . . . . By*
> *the expression "forever" it is signified that the*
> *Davidic authority and Davidic kingdom or rule*
> *over Israel shall never be taken from David's*
> *posterity. The right to rule will never be*
> *transferred to another family, and its*
> *arrangement is designed for eternal*
> *perpetuity.*[10]

One of the difficulties in which Armstrong entangles himself is that of not recognizing the fact that there is a conditional aspect to the Davidic covenant. Pentecost declares:

> *The only conditional element in the covenant*
> *was whether the descendants of David would*
> *continually occupy the throne or not.*

> *Disobedience might bring about chastening, but*
> *never abrogate the covenant.*[11]

Armstrong is very quick to use Psalm 89:3-4 to demonstrate that the covenant made with David cannot be broken. However, he would seem to ignore verses 38-39 which would indicate that God has forestalled the blessings of such a covenant. Perowne, in his commentary, declares:

> *But now comes the mournful contrast. This*
> *covenant made by God, confirmed and ratified*
> *by an oath, eternal as the heavens are eternal,*
> *sure as the order of the universe is sure—what*
> *has become of it? Has it not failed, or is it not in*
> *danger of failing? Appearances are against its*
> *perpetuity, against the truth of God. The*
> *expostulation of the Psalmist is nothing less*
> *than a reproach. God has with His own hand*
> *cast down the throne of David, and annulled the*
> *covenant: so it seems to one who measures*
> *promise and performance by a human*
> *standard.*[12]

The following verses may be the answer to the unheeding Israelite who neglected the warning of Scripture.

> *That Jehovah may establish his word which he*
> *spake concerning me saying, If thy children take*
> *heed to their way, to walk before me in the truth*
> *with all their heart and with all their soul, there*
> *shall not fail thee (said he) a man on the throne*
> *of Israel. (1 Kings 2:4)*

To any student of the Old Testament it is known that Israel did not heed this warning; thus the physical throne was later taken from and removed to be filled in yet a future time by the person of Jesus Christ.[13]

Perhaps the finishing reproof of the physical perpetuity of the Davidic throne is contained within the words of Scripture itself. The prophet Hosea declares:

> For the children of Israel shall abide many days without king, and without prince, and without sacrifice, and without pillar, and without ephod or teraphim: afterward shall the children of Israel return, and seek Jehovah their God, and David their king, and shall come with fear unto Jehovah and to his goodness in the latter days. (Hos. 3:4-5)

It is not within the confines of this paper to trace the genealogies of the Israelites to the country of Ireland, Scotland and ultimately to England. In resume, Armstrong uses Scripture, Irish folklore and history to prove that the prophet Jeremiah transplanted the throne of David to England. This was done by bringing with himself the daughter of King Zedekiah.[14] Her name is said in Armstrong lore to be Tea-Tephi. Simply let it be stated that in the entire 226 pages of Armstrong's work, *The United States and British Commonwealth in Prophecy*, there is not one footnote to substantiate the historical claims which give solidarity to his Anglo-Israelite theory.

The Claim of Geography

In this section, the writer wishes to deal primarily with ground, land, countries and a direction which brought the ten lost tribes to Great Britain. How British-Israelism can twist Scripture to present to the world the fact that they had a land already chosen by God is a mystery. The basis of the British-Israel theory *assumes* certain things which are contrary to fact. They assume that these deported captives began to wander from the place of their exile and went westward through northern Europe and became the ancestors of the Saxons, who later invaded England. Thus, the theory is that the

Anglo-Saxons are the lost ten tribes. This means that white, English-speaking people are really the chosen people of God.

One would expect that a theory of such magnitude would have a historical basis. This is not the case, however. There is another view that some members of the lost tribes made their way toward Denmark, and from Denmark some went on to England. Another group of wanderers from the tribe of Dan followed Jeremiah to Ireland in the sixth century B.C., among them Tea-Tephi, who they claim was the daughter of Zedekiah, the last king of Judah. The story goes that she fell in love with Heremon, king of Ireland, and they were married. A list of names are then presented, from where no one knows, to indicate that Queen Victoria is a descendant of this pair, and through this daughter of Zedekiah, the throne of David moved from Jerusalem to Great Britain.[15]

To the best knowledge of this writer, in any writing published, there is positively no evidence that Zedekiah had a daughter who ever went to Ireland. Nor do we have any historical documentated material that there ever was a person by the name of Tea-Tephi. Agreed, ancient ballads speak of an Irish Queen named Tea and a British Queen with the name of Tephi, but this is not history. This is mere speculation.

Space does not allow the writer to go into detail with the genealogy of Zedekiah. For information only as far as geography, it is a well known fact that there is no reliable Irish history until several centuries after Christ. No respectable scholar will for a moment take seriously these outlandish claims by Anglo-Israel theorists or even to accept Armstrong's teaching that the "isles" (Islands) of the Bible refer to the British Isles.

A book called Judah's *Sceptre and Joseph's Birthright* was loaned to this author by one of the officials of the Anglo-Saxon Federation. In the front of this book is a map showing Europe and the Near East and with a line drawn northwest from Jerusalem to the British Isles. Underneath the map is this explanatory quotation from the forty-ninth chapter of Isaiah (see Appendix J):

> *Behold, these [Israel in the Isles] shall come*
> *from far, and lo, these from the north and from*

> *the west. The children which thou shalt have,*
> *after thou hast lost the other, shall say again in*
> *thine ears, The place is too straight [cramped]*
> *for me, give a place to me that I may dwell. (Isa.*
> *49:12,20)*

> *Overlooking what has been here added to the*
> *Word of God in the brackets, an examination of*
> *Isaiah 49:12 will disclose that the last part of*
> *the verse has been omitted, with no indication*
> *that an omission has been made. The verse*
> *reads, "Behold, these shall come from afar;*
> *and, lo, these from the north and from the west;*
> *and these from the land of Sinim. (Isa. 49:12)*

Why has the last part of verse 12 been omitted? Evidently because Sinim is believed by Bible students to be a land in the East, possibly China, and to have the children in the isles returning from China or the East as well as from the northwest, would be fatal to the Anglo-Israel theory at this point.[16]

British-Israelism makes much of the fact that God would "plant" his people in a particular place and that they should move no more (2 Sam. 7:10), and that this PLACE could not possibly have been Palestine because they were IN Palestine when this prophecy or promise was made.

If such is the case, then we have a flat contradiction of Genesis 15:18. The river Euphrates does not spell "Thames" (of England). Furthermore, the Thames is not a "Great" river.

Note also that God gave all the land of Canaan to Abraham and to his SEED for an EVERLASTING possession. Again, we iterate, Canaan does not spell E-n-g-l-a-n-d.[17]

Add to all that has been said to the prophecy of Hosea: "For the children of Israel shall abide many days without a king and without a prince, and without a sacrifice, and without an image, and without an ephod, and without teraphim" (Hos. 3:4). Right here you have conclusive proof that there is no need or purpose in transplanting and transferring the throne to Ireland, Scotland, England or any other place until Messiah Himself comes to fulfill the promise and to sit upon the throne of his father, David, forever (Luke 1:32-33).

The Philological Claim

British-Israelites do considerable violence to philology generally. Dr. J. A. Vaus, Director of the Hebrew Department of the Bible Institute, says, "A religious system that seeks to justify its claims by an appeal to resemblances in words of different languages, succeeds only in displaying the poverty of its proofs."[18]

On the surface it seems that what the British-Israelites say about language is true, but they do not fool those of us who have had Hebrew and Greek. There is absolutely no connection between the Hebrew language and the Anglo-Saxon tongue.

As we look into the past pages of history, we come to the conclusion that no immigration of a vast horde, especially of the children of Israel, has ever occurred without carrying with it language, customs, physiognomy, synagogues and circumcision.

British-Israelism supposes that two or three million Israelites poured into the British Isles, somehow dropping everything—language, physiognomy, records, customs and their names. The entire lack of evidence simply means that the event alleged never occurred.

It is strange that the entire race which once wrote from right to left should (without government compulsion, which would have been impossible), silently, unanimously, with no conceivable motive, and leaving not a single trace of the process behind—thus revolutionize its penmanship by now writing from left to right. This is one of the most remarkable fantasies.[19]

Again and again we are assured by British-Israelism that the Hebrew language is closely related to Keltic and Anglo-Saxon, and that there are many names which clearly prove their identity with Israel. But the actual evidence could hardly be any weaker. Almost any language can show occasional sounds and syllables which remind one of Hebrew. For this reason, such utterly groundless arguments are presented as the following: "Brithish"(contracted to British), a pure Hebrew word. "Brith" occurs over a hundred times in the Old Testament and is always translated "covenant." "Ish" is the Hebrew word for "man,"[20] and it also appears many times in Scripture. Hence, Brithish or British signifies the "covenant people." It is true that brith signifies "covenant" in Hebrew, and aish "man," but it does not follow that aish means people. "Aish" cannot apply to a people or covenant people, but a man. (אִישׁ)[21] But surely ish here, as in many other English words, is simply the adjective termination. "Childish" does not signify child-man! And it is better to have a childlike trust in God's Word than in such childish derivations. German has this termination, but not Hebrew.[22]

This is what Dr. Lawrence Duff Forbes has to say about the claim that "British" means "man of the covenant."

But hold! There is a fly in the ointment! Since the word "covenant" possesses no adjectival force in Hebrew, the two nouns are in what is known as the construct state. So placed, the meaning would be "a man of a covenant," but even for this concept, it should rather be "Ish HaBrith." Thus, to get even remotely near this philological monstrosity, we would require to reverse the order of the words.

The B/I (British-Israel) balderdash based on "British," if it proves anything, proves too much. For what of the word "Britain"? Permitting this author a similar use of assonance, may it be remarked that "Ain" in Hebrew is a particle of negation, meaning "not" or "without." It is so translated in Hosea 3:4, "ain meleck," "without a king," etc. Thus, if "British" is "covenant-man," then "Brit-ain" is "without a covenant"!

Professor U. H. Parker, professor of Hebrew at McMaster University, Hamilton, Ontario, has already pointed out the unscholarly gasconade of British-Israelism in this direction. Of the words, "British" and "Britain," he says:

> *These words are not Hebrew, nor has any Hebrew*
> *scholar ever supposed them to be such. "Britain"*

is an ancient Celtic or West-Germanic term. It appears in its cognate form, in the classics, and was handed down to modern England via both Old English and Latin. Incidentally, it is really the plural of "Briton." "British" is simply the old Celtic "Bret" (a Briton) plus the familiar suffix "ish," which is used to form adjectives of common Teutonic origin. This suffix is cognate with the German "isc," the Dutch "isch" and the Greek "iskos." To persist, as some do, in seeking to identify it with the Hebrew word "eesh" (man) might well be described as mulish, childish, and foolish.

British-Israelites do considerable violence to philology generally. They weave a fanciful tale that "Isaac's sons" is really the basis of the word "Saxons." The full humor of this can only be appreciated by a Hebrew scholar! If it is really legitimate to thus ride from one nationality to another by saddling an assonance, could we not equally prove that the inhabitants of Hamburg were mountaineers of negro origin violating the Jewish dietary laws?[23]

Again warning against the vagaries of B/I, Professor Parker declares:

As a matter of fact, there are hardly more than two dozen words, exclusive of Bible names, in the English vocabulary which can be traced to Hebrew roots . . . . Nearly every one of the Hebrew words we do have come to us via the Greeks and might more reasonably be credited to the Phoenicians than to Hebrew.[24]

This writer could give many examples of this kind of pseudo-scholarship among the proponents of the British-Israel view, but two more will suffice. To follow the movements of the tribe of Dan and to prove that it was among those that settled in Ireland, British-Israelism points to the many instances that a "din," "dun" or "don" is part of the name of a territory, city or river where they supposedly passed through or settled. A few of the names mentioned are: Macedonia, Dardanelles, Danube, Denmark, Dunbar, London, etc. However, several students have pointed out that using this same kind of reasoning, we could establish that the tribe of Dan went to Africa where are the Danakil and Dinka tribes, where the Donalists are a Christian cult, and where one can find Dondo and Denkera. Any imaginative person could present a wonderful case for the settling of each of the tribes in areas all over the world if he does with their names what the Anglo-Israelites do with Dan.[25]

Still more ridiculous is the explanation that the word "Saxon" is also Hebrew and that it means Isaac's sons. The Anglo-Israelites claim that each Britisher is an Isaac son. Anyone claiming correspondence between the Hebrew term "Isaac's son" and "Saxon" is woefully ignorant of the Hebrew. Isaac in Hebrew is Yitshak, and son is ben. Isaac's son is Ben Yitshak(בֶּן יִצְחָק). And in the (LXX, Ἰσαάκ). There is absolutely no similarity in sound between these two words. Also, we never read in Scripture, *sons* of Isaac, for he had only one son whom God recognized.[26]

Israel vs Judah

As a Hebrew-Christian, this author is furious at the lack of scholarship and injustice to the Scriptures Armstrong carries as to the words "Jew," "Hebrew," "Israel" and "Judah." With no intent to offend any British-Israelite as an individual, the claims they make are untrue, unscriptural and unfounded. To deny that the ten tribes crucified Jesus and to put the blame on the Jews and Romans is without merit. Hear Peter at Pentecost: "Therefore, let ALL the House of Israel know assuredly that God hath made that same Jesus, whom ye have crucified, both Lord and Christ" (Acts 2:36).

It is "Jews" out of "every nation under heaven" whom Peter means when he says, "ye men of Israel," and to whom the charge is leveled.

As Jesus used Scripture to refute the devil when He was tempted, the writer will do the same to refute the concept of Armstrong that the term "Israel" never refers to the Jews both in Old Testament history and New Testament quotations. Kittel perhaps answers the question in part by saying:

> At any rate, Israel is originally a sacral term. It denotes the totality of the elect of Yahweh and those united in the Yahweh cult. It thus embraces the central beliefs of the league. The rise of the monarchy puts an end to the sacral league. It thus brings about a change in the use of the name Israel . . . .
>
> The fall of the northern kingdom and the deportation of 722 introduced a new change in the significance and use of the name Israel, and the third phase dates from this point. Israel is now adopted by the southern kingdom and it is used again for the whole of God's people as a spiritual designation which transcends such political titles as the house of Judah or the province of Judah.
>
> This use of Israel even for the southern kingdom had deep roots, for Judah was once a member of the great tribal league, and then part of the greater Davidic kingdom. Even in the later monarchy the prophets could still refer to the two houses (kingdoms) of Israel (Isa. 8:14). It was thus logical that after 722 the name Israel should come to the southern kingdom with all its doctrinal implications. Both Isaiah and Micah—

immediately after 722—see that the situation has altered and use Israel for the southern kingdom (Isa. 5:7, 8:18; Mi. 2:12; 8,9; 4:14; 5:1). The name Jacob was also transferred from the northern to the southern kingdom (Mi. 2:7; 3:1, 8,9; 5:6; Na. 2:3; Isa. 2:5; 29:22). This use of the term, not as a political title, but as the name of the people of God as such, becomes normative for subsequent generations in spite of political and geographical changes.[27]

Kittell further asserts in his monumental work:

Both terms denote a people. That is to say, they describe individuals in terms of their genealogical membership of this people irrespective of their national allegiance or residence. . . .

The terms and Iousaios thus express both national and religious allegiance. The two are always implied, though the emphasis may fall sometimes on the one and sometimes on the other according to the context.[28]

As if this were not enough evidence, the New Testament offers ample support that the terms are used interchangeably. Baron uses three passages to point out this significant fact:

1. In Matthew 10, Jesus sent the twelve apostles to the lost sheep of the house of Israel. The journeys of the twelve did not carry them beyond the limits of Palestine, but the "Jews" dwelling in it are regarded as the house of Israel, although many members of that "house" were also scattered in other lands.

2. On the first day of Pentecost, Peter addressed the "men of Judea"

and the great multitude from among the dispersed "Jews," as "Ye men of Israel." It would appear that Paul knew of no lost tribes after the thirteenth chapter of Acts. Although a Jew of the dispersion, he addresses them as "Men of Israel" (Acts 13:16).

3. Contained in Romans 9-11 is perhaps the most notable portion dealing with the nation of Israel. There would not seem to be a vestige or hint of a "lost Israel," apart from the one nation whose whole history Paul summarizes from the beginning to the end.[29] It may be interestingly noted that in all of Armstrong's writings concerning national eschatology, a conspicuous absence of New Testament passages is apparent. It is perhaps explainable when we realize that the New Testament supplies answers which Armstrong wishes to ignore.

The necessity of having a succinct distinction between Judah and Israel will now become apparent.

Ezra 6:17 reads concerning the offering made upon the altar of the restored temple, "Twelve he-goats for the twelve tribes of Israel." It would appear that a sacrifice for a remnant of each returning tribe was given as a commemoration of the restored temple. The prophecy of Jeremiah 51:5 says, "Israel hath not been forsaken, nor Judah of his God, . . . flee out of the midst of Babylon." Demonstrable proof that the prophets did not say that all of Judah or all of Israel, but that only a remnant of Judah and a remnant of Israel would return.

Darms asserts:

> *Enough of the ten tribes of Israel returned with Judah to warrant Ezra and Nehemiah using the terms "Israel" and "Jew" interchangeably. "Israel" appears in these two books sixty-two times, whereas "Jew" appears but nineteen times. Even the larger and more inclusive term "children of Israel" is used six times in Ezra and ten times in Nehemiah.[30]*

Even if one were to hold that none of the ten tribes returned, there was a sufficient mingling even before the captivities. Note that following the cleavage of the northern and southern kingdom, there were those who left the northern kingdom to join Judah in the south. This was especially evident during times of spiritual awakening in Judah, as during Asa's reformation (2 Chron. 15:1-10; 1 Kings 15:17, 22; 2 Chron. 16:1,6).[31]

For background information one needs to deal with Genesis 1-11 which is a record of God's working with people on a world-wide scale. Genesis 12 brings about a change in God's program. He chose one man, Abraham. The name "Hebrew" was first used in reference to Abraham (Gen. 14:13). A new term came into being with Abraham's grandson, Jacob (Gen. 32). This records the change of Jacob's name to "Israel" (v. 28). Thus, the Israelites, or children of Israel, were the descendants of Jacob. Since they were also the descendants of Abraham, it would be legitimate to refer to them both as "Hebrews" and "Israelites."

A third term comes in here in relation to one of Jacob's sons, Judah (Gen. 29:35). The name "Jew" was derived from the tribe "Judah" and was first used in 2 Kings 16:6. A member of this tribe was called a "Jew"; as a descendant of Jacob he was also an "Israelite." And as a descendant of Abraham he was also a "Hebrew."

Dr. W. W. Orr defines Jew in the following statement:

> *The name "Jew" technically refers only to one tribe, that of Judah. Abraham was originally called a Hebrew, from a term meaning to cross over. The name Israelite comes, of course, from the new name of Jacob. However, the name Jew has come to mean both Hebrew or Israelite. It is so used in the New Testament. The Jew today, therefore, is any descendant of Abraham through Isaac. Other children of Abraham are Arabs. God's program for the Jews is only through Isaac (Gen. 21:12; Rom. 9:7).[32]*

This certainly disproves Armstrong's statement in his book, *The*

United States and British Commonwealth in Prophecy. "Remember that the term 'Jew' is merely a nickname for 'Judah.' Hence, it applies to the one nation, or House of Judah only—never to the House of Israel."[33]

Part of the distinction between the names "Israel" and "Judah" was brought about by the division of the kingdom. Following this division, the name "Israel" referred to the ten northern tribes and "Judah" referred to the two southern tribes.

Basically, the name Israel belongs to all of the sons of Jacob and their descendants, when viewed from the spiritual standpoint. The "house of Israel" is used of the whole nation, including Judah, before the days of the division more than a dozen times (Ex. 16:31, 40:38; Lev. 10:6; Num. 20:29; Jos. 21:45; Ruth 4:11; 1 Sam. 7:2,3; 2 Sam. 1:12, 6:5-15, 12:8, 16:3). This is the natural and usual meaning to which the Scriptures constantly return. The term "Israel" is the spiritual title given to Jacob at Peniel (Gen. 32:28, 35:10,21,22), which applies to all his descendants, only temporarily restricted to the ten tribes, but used as in the ninth chapter of Romans of all the tribes.[34]

British-Israelism maintains that the people who returned to rebuild the temple and walls of Jerusalem were only those of the House of Judah. However, the return from captivity was not limited to Judah. The ten tribes had been taken to Assyria, and Jehovah turned the heart of the king of Assyria to strengthen their hands in the work of the house of God, the God of Israel (Ezra 6:22). It was the sons of Israel who had returned from the deportation who kept the festival (Ezra 6:21). None of the tribes were forgotten when twelve he-goats were offered, "according to the number of the tribes of Israel" (Ezra 6:17). There was a considerable "residue" of Israel (Neh. 11:20) in the restoration. All of these were called "Jews," not because they were all of the tribe of Judah, but because they associated themselves with that tribe, under its religious and political leadership, because it upheld the worship of Jehovah in Jerusalem, His appointed place[35] (see Appendix I).

Again, David Baron, the noted Jewish authority, is quoted:

The name Jew and Israelite became synonymous

> *terms from about the time of captivity. It is one*
> *of the absurd fallacies of Anglo-Israelism to*
> *suppose that the term Jew stands for a bodily*
> *descendant of Judah. It stands for all of those*
> *from among the sons of Jacob who acknowledge*
> *themselves subject in the Kingdom of Israel.*
> *Anglo-Israelism teaches that the members of the*
> *ten tribes are never called "Jews" and that Jews*
> *are not Israelites; but both assertions are false.*
> *In the New Testament the same people that are*
> *called Jews one hundred seventy-four times are*
> *also called Israel no fewer than seventy-five*
> *times.*[36]

The evidence of *only* Judah going back to rebuild is over and over again refuted by Scripture. Ezra refers to God's people as Israelites forty times and as Jews eight times. Nehemiah refers to God's people as Israelites twenty-two times and as Jews eleven times. If "Jew" refers only to a person of the tribe of Judah and never to all Israelites, then the return of the Jews from Babylon would not be considered a return of "all Israel." Yet, the words, "all Israel," are used in Ezra 2:70, 6:17, 8:25,35, 10:5; Nehemiah 7:73, 12:47. From these passages alone it is evident that the terms "Jew" and "Israel" were used interchangeably at this time.

Paul referred to himself as being "of the tribe of Benjamin," yet he called himself "an Hebrew of the Hebrews" (Phil. 3:5). In Acts 21:39 and 22:3, Paul makes these statements: "I am a man which am a Jew of Tarsus," and "I am verily a man which am a 'Jew.'" Then in 2 Cor. 11:22 he refers to himself as an Israelite: "Are they Hebrews? So am I. Are they Israelites? So am I. Are they the seed of Abraham? So am I."

Nicodemus, who came to Jesus by night, is described both as a "ruler of the Jews" and a "master in Israel" (John 3:1,10). The famous Pharisee, Gamaliel, addressed the apostles as "men of Israel" (Acts 5:35).

If the term "Jew" refers only to the House of Judah, as the teachers of British-Israelism claim, then Christ was not my Messiah, or King of the nation of Israel, but only of the tribe of Judah, for the Bible refers to Christ as the "King of the Jews. "

The sign on the cross said, "This is Jesus the King of the Jews" (Matt. 27:37). The chief priests said, "If he be the King of Israel, let him now come down from the cross" (v. 42). This shows that these leaders of Judaism used these terms interchangeably.

If the earnest student will weigh carefully every passage in the Greek Scriptures in which Israel is mentioned, he will come to the conclusion that the term always includes the whole nation, and is never limited to the ten tribes in this part of God's revelation. The reason is evident. As an independent nation, the rival of Judah, the ten tribes no longer exist. They were dispersed, not only among the gentile nations, but many of them went over to Judah at the time of the division; others joined later, and many had been left in the land and these also fell to Judah. In this way, seeing that Benjamin remained with them and most of Levi clung to them as well, it is more than probably that actual descendants of Judah were in the minority in the land, and it was far more correct to call them Israel even though many of the ten tribes, as well as the two, were dispersed among the nations even at that time.[37]

From Scripture alone one sees the fallacy that exists in British-Israelism. Somehow or other they want to fit Great Britain and the United States into the pages of the Bible, which results in many unusual, unscriptural and unethical interpretations.

Great Britain is the Ten Lost Tribes of Israel

The notion of the "lost ten tribes" of Israel has come down to us from the Middle Ages, and much theory has been woven around it. Many peoples have been "identified" as the lost ten tribes. In the seventeenth century, it was suggested that the English were of Israelitish origin. This has since been taken up by a number of writers, and has developed into what is now termed "British-Israelism."

In the preface to the book, The Lost Tribes a Myth, the author says:

> *Dr. William Rosenau, considering "What*
> *Happened to the Ten Tribes" [in Hebrew Union*
> *College Jubilee Volume (1925), pp. 79-88],*
> *decides that the Ten Tribes never were lost nor*
> *thought of by the Prophets as lost.*[38]

The house of Israel was not lost physically but spiritually, and when He came to the lost sheep of the house of Israel, He found them in Palestine and not in Britain. In the Book of Matthew, we find the twelve disciples commissioned by the Lord. What were their marching orders? Listen: "These twelve Jesus sent forth, and commanded them, saying, Go not into the way of the Gentiles, and into any city of the Samaritans enter not: But go rather to the lost sheep of the house of Israel" (Matt. 10:5-6).

They were not sent to the lost sheep of the house of Judah only, but to the lost sheep of the house of Israel. Where did they find the lost sheep of the house of Israel? In Britain? In Denmark? In the Dardanelles? In Ireland? Surely not! They were in Palestine; and to the twelve tribes the twelve disciples ministered. Numbers in the Bible have a significance, and the disciples were twelve in number, representing the twelve tribes of Israel. The fact that the twelve disciples were sent by the Lord to the house of Israel gives evidence that the twelve tribes were in the land of Palestine at the time (see Appendix K).

There is no question about the fact that the ten tribes of Israel were taken captive by Assyria. It is also true that the tribe of Judah was taken captive by Babylon, but if you look at a map (see Appendix F), you will find that the Assyrian and Babylonian empires covered essentially the same area. Therefore, the people of Jerusalem and surrounding cities were taken to the same general area that the other tribes had been taken to before them.

The Scripture often used by British-Israelites to support their claim that all Israel was taken captive is 2 Kings 17:18: "Therefore the Lord was very angry with Israel, and removed them out of his sight. There was none left but the tribe of Judah only."

If one were to stop with this verse, it would seem that no one was left except the tribe of Judah, but we must look at another portion of Scripture and notice that the tribes of Levi and Benjamin were also left behind.

> *And the king went up into the house of the Lord, and all the men of Judah, and the inhabitants of Jerusalem, and the priests, and the Levites, and all the people, great and small: and he said in their ears all the words of the book of the covenant that was found in the house of the Lord. (2 Chron. 34:30)*

> *And he caused all that were present in Jerusalem and Benjamin to stand to it. And the inhabitants of Jerusalem did according to the covenant of God, the God of their fathers. (2 Chron. 34:32)*

Therefore, the passage in question must be interpreted as referring to Judah as a kingdom and an end to Israel as a separate people. This did not mean an end to the ten tribes or being lost. However, the following Scriptures will bring to bear a definite understanding that the ten tribes were never lost and therefore could not be Great Britain.

We are told in Amos 9:9: "For, lo, I will command, and I will sift the house of Israel among all nations, like as corn is sifted in a sieve, yet shall not the last grain fall upon the earth."

This is explicit and by no means fits the teaching being examined, for Israel is to be sifted among all nations, not simply a few lands for a part of the time. This tells us very plainly where the "lost ten tribes" are. They, like the Jews, are dispersed, not gathered; they are scattered, not in one place; each one of them is separated from the rest as grain is by a sieve, so that each falls in a separate location. Here we have clear intimations which answer the questions as to the "lost ten tribes." They are not "lost," they are scattered. They are not gathered as a nation or a company of nations, but are to be found as individuals among all nations. We have all come into contact with them under the name of "Jew." Only in Palestine are they striving to come together again in order to become a nation. And only there will they have a national existence after they are gathered and joined with Judah.

The Testimony of Assyrian Inscriptions

There is not a word of truth in the theory that when the northern kingdom of Israel fell, all the people were carried into Assyrian captivity. The Bible makes it plain—they were not. In 721 B.C., the ten tribes were defeated by the Assyrians, and a number of the most talented people were taken captive. The Old Testament does not tell us exactly how many were deported, but an inscription by Sargon II, who succeeded Shalmaneser V, makes it clear that most of the Israelites were not taken to Assyria:

> *I besieged and conquered Samaria [Sa-me-ri-na], led away as booty 27,290 inhabitants of it. I formed among them a contingent of 50 chariots and made remaining [inhabitants] assume their [social] positions. I installed over them an office of mine and imposed upon them the tribute of the former king.[39]*

> *At the beginning [of my rule . . . the city of the Sa] Marious I [besieged and conquered . . .] who let me achieve my victory . . . carried off prisoner (27,290 of the people who dwelt in it; from among them I equipped 50 chariots for my royal army units . . . the City of Samaria). I restored and made it more habitable than before. (I brought into it) people of the countries conquered by my own hands. (My official I set over them as district-governor and) imposed upon them tribute as on an Assyrian (city) . . . I made to mix with each other; the market price . . . . (Annals, 10-18).[40]*

This inscription indicates definitely that the vast majority of the ten tribes were left in their own land under rulers appointed by Assyria. The natives of the northern kingdom continued to be in the majority and many of them placed themselves under the rule of Judah. This fact is confirmed that one hundred years later we see a great number of people joined in the religious festivals of Hezekiah and Josiah.

EVIDENCE OF THE PRESENCE OF ISRAEL

Israel Attends the Passover of Hezekiah

In his zeal to have a religious revival, Hezekiah sent invitations to *all* the people of the Lord to attend a passover. It is imperative at this point for British-Israelism to note that Ephraim and Manasseh are mentioned in particular: "And Hezekiah sent to all Israel and Judah, and wrote letters also to Ephraim and Manasseh, that they should come to the Lord at Jerusalem, to keep the passover unto the Lord God of Israel" (2 Chron. 30:1).

The messengers bearing this invitation were instructed to cover all the area of original Israel—Dan to Beer-Sheba—and to invite all Judah and Israel as we will see in the following Scriptures:

> *So they established a decree to make proclamation throughout all Israel, from Beersheba even to Dan, that they should come to keep the passover unto the Lord God of Israel at Jerusalem: for they had not done it of a long time. So the posts went with the letters from the king and his princes throughout all Israel and Judah, and according to the commandment of the king, saying, ye children of Israel, turn again unto the Lord God of Abraham, Isaac, and Israel, and he will return to the remnant of you, that are escaped out of the hand of the kings of*

> *Assyria (2 Chron. 30:5-6).*

> *So the posts passed from city to city through the country of Ephraim and Manasseh even unto Zebulun; but they laughed them to scorn, and mocked them. Nevertheless divers of Ashu and Manasseh and of Zebulun humbled themselves, and came to Jerusalem (2 Chron. 30:10-11).*

Israel Attends the Passover of Josiah

Among those contributing money for the repair of the Temple by Josiah are those of "Manasseh and Ephraim, and all the remnant of Israel" (2 Chron. 34:9). The record of Scripture affirms that Israel was represented at this passover also as they had been under Hezekiah.

> *And the children of Israel that were present kept the passover at that time; and the feast of unleavened bread seven days. And there was no passover like to that kept in Israel from the days of Samuel the prophet; neither did all the kings of Israel keep such a passover as Josiah kept, and the priests, and the Levites, and all Judah and Israel that were present, and the inhabitants of Jerusalem (2 Chron. 35:17-18).*

Israel Returns From Babylon

If the British-Israelites will read carefully the Book of Ezra, they will see that all the children of Israel, some from every tribe, returned. In the first chapter, verse 3, we read: "Who is there among you of all his people? His God be with him, and let him go up to Jerusalem, which is in Judah, and build the house of the Lord God of Israel, which (he is God) is in Jerusalem."

In Ezra 2:70 we read of the priests:

And the Levites, and some of the people who
"dwelt in their cities, and all Israel in their
cities." The inspired writer could have used the
word "Jews."

Also in Ezra we read:

And the children of Israel, the priests, and the
Levites, and the rest of the children of the
captivity, kept the dedication of this house of
God with joy, and offered at the dedication of
this house of God an hundred bullocks, two
hundred rams, four hundred lambs; and for a
sin offering for all Israel, twelve he-goats,
according to the number of the tribes of Israel
(Ezra 6:16-17).

In Ezra 7:28 the writer says, "And I gathered together out of Israel chief men to go up with me." Notice he does not say that just Judah or Benjamin went up with him, but "out of Israel chief men." Knowing that if those who claim that the ten tribes were lost would read the entire Book of Ezra with care, and exegete the Scriptures properly, you will see that some of all the tribes were there.

If the ten tribes were not included in this Scripture by Ezra, then they were not of "all the people." When the Temple was dedicated, those doing it were not two-tribed Judah, but twelve-tribed Israel.

If the "lost sheep of the house of Israel" is Great Britain, then Jesus failed. The ministry of Jesus and the Twelve was confined to Galilee, Judea and Perea and a brief trip into Samaria, so how could Israel be in the isles? And if Judah or the Jews are not also to be identified as the "lost sheep of the house of Israel," then Jesus spent His ministry among the wrong people.

The Evidence of the New Testament

The New Testament testifies to the fact that the ten tribes were not erased from the face of the earth. Anna the prophetess was said to be of the tribe of Asher (Luke 2:36), which shows strong evidence of a remaining Israelite population. If the Assyrian deportation of the tribes was in toto, then it would have been impossible for the genealogy of Anna to have survived.

The Apostle Paul never considered the disappearance of the tribes. He told King Agrippa, "and now I stand and am judged for the hope of the promise made of God unto our Father; unto which promise our twelve tribes, instantly serving God day and night, hope to come" (Acts 26:6-7). In Acts 2:22, Peter addressed "ye men of Israel." And again in Acts 3:12, he said, "ye men of Israel, why marvel ye at this man?" Acts 4:10, "be it known unto you all, and to all the people of Israel." Acts 5:21, "But the high priest came in and called the council together, and all the senate of the Children of Israel." In the Book of James 1:1, the writer addressed his letter to "the twelve tribes which are scattered abroad." The Book of Revelation, chapter 7:4-8, tells of the saving of 12,000 people from each of the twelve tribes of Israel.

If the true Israelites, the inheritors of the promises, were dwelling in the area of Great Britain at this time, as British-Israelism states, then Peter was mistaken in promising the Jews that the kingdom would be established if they received Jesus Christ.

Evidence From Archaeology

Archaeological evidence indicates that the "remnant" mentioned in 2 Chron. 34:9 was not a small group. According to recent archaeological findings, as the northern kingdom fell, thousands of refugees fled south to Judah in order to escape the Assyrians. Dr. Magen Broshi, an archaeologist at the Israel Museum, in a recent study, made the following statement as to the increased population of the city of Jerusalem:

It is becoming increasingly clear that Jerusalem
underwent a major expansion during the eighth
century B.C. Most of the evidence of this
expansion comes from Israeli excavations in the
city since 1968. In 1970, Professor Nachman
Avigad found a massive wall between 20 and 23
feet wide on the western ridge, which he dates
toward the end of the eighth century. Beneath
this wall, and therefore earlier than it, Professor
Avigad found a structure which may date
somewhat earlier in the eighth century,
indicating that the western expansion of the city
started before the building of the wall there.
Excavations west of the wall indicate that by the
end of the eighth century, Jerusalem had
extensive suburbs outside the city wall.[41]

Other excavations also revealed evidence of initial occupation during this period. All of this makes it clear, in Dr. Broshi's words, "that Jerusalem at about 700 B.C., had mushroomed, historically speaking, overnight." From the death of Solomon to the end of the eighth century B.C.—almost two hundred years—the city limits changed very little. Then toward the end of the eighth century the city expanded by a factor of three or four. Dr. Broshi estimates the population of the city increased from about 7,500 to about 24,000.

Dr. Broshi states that the evidence for an influx of refugees is not confined to Jerusalem. In 1967 and 1968, a survey conducted by Professor Moshe Kochani of Tel Aviv University revealed that almost half of the settlements were founded during the century before the First Temple was finally destroyed in 587 B.C. Other scholars have found numerous settlements in the Negev, in the Judean desert and along the Dead Sea were heavily settled for the first time in the eighth century B.C. According to Dr. Broshi, the Israelites from the northern kingdom fled, not only to Jerusalem, but also to numerous other sites in Judah. In this way, large numbers of people from the "lost tribes" of Israel melded into the population of their sister kingdom of Judah.[42]

The Evidence at Shechem

G. Ernest Wright shows that the reoccupation of Shechem after the retaliation of Shalmanessar against the conspiracy of Hoshea is represented by Stratum Six. He notes that, "The presence of foreigners in the country is attested by a considerable quantity of 'Assyrian Palace Ware,' a pottery which followed Mesopotamian models, though most of it was locally made. Yet little of Stratum Six remains."[43] But the critical conclusion of the examination of the pottery of Stratum Six is, "The fact that most of the pottery follows earlier Palestinian tradition, except for the bowls made on Mesopotamia models, indicates that not all the people of the reoccupation were foreigners by any means."[44]

The Evidence of Samaria

It is entirely probable that the capture of Samaria by the Assyrians and the partial deportation of the inhabitants replaced by new settlers from elsewhere, would introduce a number of new forms of pottery which would be found, together with wares resembling those of the earlier period.[45]

Having established on the basis of Bible history, Scripture and archaeological findings that the ten tribes were never lost and that the Jews represent all the tribes of Israel, we must reject the theory that Great Britain is the Lost Tribes of Israel.

Race vs Grace

According to Armstrong, birthright has to do with race, not grace.[46] It is acquired simply by being born. This reminds the author of a young Methodist minister in our town who, when asked the question,"When did you become a Christian?" said, "I can't remember the time I wasn't a Christian."

The Jews have always believed in salvation by race. The writer's mother and father are Orthodox Jews who believe this today. They are going to heaven because they are of the seed of Abraham.

Again we find British-Israelism misinterpreting Scripture. There seems to be a "new Galatinism" which says that a man must obey not only the Gospel, but the law of Moses as well to be saved. Let us go back to Genesis 12, where the Lord promised He would do four things for Abraham.

1. God declared that He would produce from His servant a great nation.

2. God would bless him.

3. God would make his name great.

4. God would make him a blessing to all the families of the earth.

Each promise was literally fulfilled: the nation of Israel (twelve tribes, not ten) did descend from Abraham and through Christ, his descendants, all the families of the earth have been blessed. No one anywhere can deny this. However, when God repeated the covenant to Abraham, He added to it by promising the patriarch he would be "a father of many nations" (Gen. 17:4), and then added in verse 6 these words: "I will make thee exceedingly fruitful and I will make nations of thee, and kings shall come out of thee."

Scripture does not say only Israel, but Abraham will be the father of *many nations*. This promise, as every promise of God, was literally fulfilled through Ishmael (his son by Hagar), the six sons of Keturah, and Esau (his grandson), who also became the ancestor of numerous kings.

If we are going to deal with genealogy, let us use the Holy Scriptures for our source. Without question the greatest blessings would be centered around one *special* nation (Gen. 12:3), beyond numbering (Gen. 13:16, 15:5). God announced that He would give the seed of Isaac the land of Canaan as an everlasting possession. Granted, other descendants of Abraham are honored, but again the promise of Canaan, the "land flowing with milk and honey" was limited to *one* particular line. God specially told the patriarch, "in Isaac shall thy seed be called" (Gen. 21:12). The word of God spoke to Rebekah, Isaac's wife, that the younger of twin boys not yet born to her would receive this special promise.

And the Lord said unto her, Two nations are in thy womb, and two manner of people shall be born of thee; and the one people shall be stronger than the other people; and the elder shall serve the younger (Gen. 25:23).

Jacob's sons, not Esau, became the progenitors of the twelve tribes of Israel, which hold a special place in God's prophetic program.

Genesis 35:11, according to British-Israelism, is fulfilled in the nations that make up the Anglo-Saxon people. "A nation and *a company of nations* shall be of thee. The context, however, very definitely states that this was to be accomplished in the land of Canaan, which God "gave Abraham and Isaac and Jacob." The word "gahal" (קָהָל), here rendered "company," means "a congregation."[47] It means, according to Strong's *Exhaustive Concordance*, assembly or multitude [48] (קְהַל יִשְׂרָאֵל).[49] Gahal Yisrael means the "congregation of the people of Israel." The twelve tribes and Levi were a "congregation of nations" during all the years of their history. How Anglo-Israelites can make the statement that they *alone*, or should we get more specific and say Great Britain *alone*, has been such a "company of nations" where every empire that has come and gone, including Babylon, Persia, Greece and Rome, has been a "company of nations." The Soviet Union is also a "company of nations" today.

Much more on race, especially the chosen race, from the seed of Abraham, will be brought out in the next chapters on the dangers of British-Israelism. However, the writer would like to leave this section with the words of Paul: "And if ye be Christ's, then are ye Abraham's seed, and heirs according to the promise" (Gal. 3:29).

British-Israelism is fundamentally an abandonment of Grace for Law. To claim that blessings are based not on obedience, but on *race*, is something the Law itself never did and is profoundly hostile to Grace. Paul, in Phil. 3:8, summarizes it beautifully when he says, "summing it all up as dung."[50]

The Sabbath Claim

There are many groups who are not Hebrews, but still believe that if they keep the Sabbath, they do not steal, kill or commit adultery, they are obeying the Mosaic moral code. There are too many groups who still believe in legalism and one of these groups is British-Israelism or Armstrongism.

The following will show the error of the British-Israelism doctrine of the Sabbath.

1. The basic argument from British-Israelites for an eternal Sabbath is from the word "forever" (Ex. 31:16-17). The Hebrew word, "olam" (עוֹלָם) "forever," has as its root meaning "a long, indefinite period of time." It does not mean eternal or without end, as British-Israelism states. Often the word "olam" is used of the past, as in Gen. 6:4: "mighty men . . . of old."[51]

2. It is imperative for one to read the book of Hebrews:

> *But now hath he obtained a more excellent ministry, by how much also he is the mediator of a better covenant, which was established upon better promises. For if the first covenant had been faultless, then should no place have been sought for the second. For finding fault with them, he saith, Behold, the days come, saith the Lord, when I will make a new covenant with the house of Israel and with the house of Judah: Not according to the covenant that I made with their fathers in the day when I took them by the hand to lead them out of the land of Egypt; because they continued not in my covenant, and I regarded them not, saith the Lord. For this is the covenant that I will make with the house of Israel after those days, saith the Lord; I will put my laws into their mind, and write them in their hearts: and I will be to them a God, and they shall be to me a people (Heb. 8:6-10).*

The citation above is Jeremiah 31:31, meaning the New Testament.

3. The Sabbath was a part of the covenant made with Israel only. The Israelites were to use this day to remember that God had delivered them from Egyptian bondage (Deut. 5:15). The first day of the week is the new Lord's day. After the resurrection of Christ, we find the early Christians meeting together on the first day of the week for breaking of bread and the preaching of God's Word (Acts 20:7).

The writer must interject here that in the mind of Herbert Armstrong, however, those in the early church who did not observe the Sabbath on Saturday could not have been true Christians.[52] To him, the keeping of the Sabbath determines whether one is to be saved or lost. In his book, *Which Day is the Christian Sabbath?* he calls Sabbath keeping, "the Test Command—the one on which your very salvation and eternity depends!"[53]

The writer has found to be true as a Hebrew Christian that those who hold to the Sabbath as given to Israel usually hold to a mixture of law and grace, dietary laws and Jewish feasts. To dispel anyone who believes in salvation in a day or in a legalistic system that saves needs only to look to Paul's letter to the Galatians: "I do not frustrate the grace of God: for if righteousness come by the law, then Christ is dead in vain" (Gal. 2:21).

> *But before faith came, we were kept under the law, shut up unto the faith which should afterwards be revealed. Wherefore the law was our schoolmaster to bring us unto Christ, that we might be justified by faith. But after that faith is come, we are no longer under a schoolmaster. For ye are all the children of God by faith in Christ Jesus (Gal. 3:23-26).*

A. J. Polloch makes the following statement: "(Ex. 31:13,16,17; Ezek. 20:12-20), refers to the whole twelve tribes, and there is not a shred of reference to the ten tribes as such." He goes on to say that "the Sabbath in these proof passages refers to the seventh day of the week, and this the British nation does not keep."[54]

The outstanding Hebrew-Christian scholar, Dr. Charles L. Feinberg, who this writer has known for twenty years, makes the following statement in his book, *The Sabbath and the Lord's Day*:

> A study of 2,500 years between Adam and Moses will reveal that the institution of the Sabbath *(7] ש)is not commanded anywhere. While one finds accounts through archaeology of the rite of circumcision, the sacrifices, offering of the tithe and the institution of marriage, we find no mention of the great institution of the Sabbath. And the interesting observation is that the Sabbath is not mentioned anywhere in Genesis after its first occurrence in Genesis 2, where it refers to God alone.[55]

Many attempts have been made on the part of Seventh-Day Adventists to attribute the keeping of the Lord's Day to man. Let us check history.

Evidence From History

1. Pliny, Governor of Bithynia, Asia Minor, wrote in A.D. 107 to Trojan concerning the Christians, "They were wont to meet together, on a stated day."

2. Ignatius, who died about A.D. 110, wrote in his Epistle, "For if we still live according to Judaism we confess that we have not received grace."

3. Barnabas, A.D. 120, wrote, "Wherefore, also, we keep the eighth day with joyfulness, the day, also, on which Jesus rose again from the dead."

4. Justin Martyr, A.D. 140, wrote, "Sunday is the day on which we will hold our common assembly, because Jesus Christ Our Saviour, on the same day rose from the dead."

All available evidence shows definitely that the Lord's Day was not instituted by man, according to the Holy Bible or the early church fathers. There is a clear statement from Scripture, "This is the day the Lord hath made" (Ps. 118:24).

As a Hebrew-Christian, questions often come as to why this writer broke the Sabbath, especially from Seventh-Day Adventists. First of all, let us quote from Scripture:

> *Wherefore the children of Israel shall keep the sabbath to observe the sabbath throughout their generations, for a perpetual covenant. It is a sign between me and the children of Israel forever; for in six days the Lord made heaven and earth, and on the seventh day he rested, and was refreshed (Ex. 31:16-17).*

Here we notice that the Sabbath was a sign between Jehovah and the nation of Israel.

There is not a single Scripture to show that God ever gave the Sabbath for members of the body of Christ in this day of grace. This Hebrew-Christian writer is delivered from the law, is dead to the law, and is not under the law.

A very interesting and exhaustive examination was conducted in the Holy Scriptures. From the sin of Adam until the time Israel left Egypt, 2500 years later, there is not a word concerning the Sabbath.

In this day of grace, believing sinners find rest in a Person, not in a day and that Person is the Lord Jesus Christ. He is the Lord of the Sabbath. The Sabbath observance was a part of the Mosaic Law, which in Christ has been done away. Christ said, "I came not to destroy the Law but to fulfill the Law." You see, He was the Law. Jesus not only came to the Lost House of Israel (Twelve Tribes), but came to usher in a new order, a new covenant.

The Saturday for the Jew, the Seventh-Day Adventist, the Seventh-Day Baptist, the Worldwide Church of God (Armstrongism) is still the Sabbath, but those who are believers worship our Lord Jesus Christ on the first day of the week—the day He arose from the grave!

EXTRA BIBLICAL EVIDENCE

Introduction

The saddest feature of British-Israelism, Anglo-Israelism or Armstrongism is the deliberate attempt on the part of their writers to remodel and remake the Word of God to prove their contentions. By careful exegesis these men would see that God's Holy Word plainly states that the twelve tribes were in a dispersion in the days of the apostles (James 1:1). If descendants of the ten tribes no longer existed at the time, it would have been futile for James to address his letter to all twelve tribes. We are told precisely where some of them were dispersed (1 Peter 1:1-2). They were in various parts of Asia Minor, in Pontus, Galatia, Cappadocia, the province of Asia and in Bithynia, in such large numbers that Peter, the chief of the apostles, sent a letter to them. "The strangers scattered" (Greek, diaspora) meaning dispersion used collectively for the dispersed Jews after the Babylonian captivity.

Notice very carefully the following verses taken out of context by British-Israelites.

> *That in blessing I will bless thee, and in*
> *multiplying I will multiply thy seed as the stars*
> *of the heaven, and as the sand which is upon the*
> *seashore; and thy seed shall possess the gate of*
> *his enemies (Gen. 22:17).*

How in the world can this passage mean Britain? There are no parallels between Israel's promises and the blessings now upon the Anglo-Saxon peoples.

In Hebrew there are a great many idioms used. It seems that the British-Israelites cannot recognize this or understand that this passage is merely saying that the promised seed of Abraham through Isaac would defeat its enemies and conquer the land of Palestine. This is not a prophetic picture of the British people or the United States controlling Gibraltar,

Malta, Suez or Singapore. In this text, as with many others, Anglo-Israelites take the glory that belongs to Jesus Christ and ascribe it to Great Britain, and its king.

Now anyone with any integrity for the Word of God would certainly use Galatians 3:16 as a cross reference. Paul tells us in this passage who the seed is that God mentions. "Now to Abraham and his seed were the promises made. He saith not, and to seeds, as of many, but as of one, and to thy seed, which is *Christ*."

Christ, the Messiah of Israel, is the one to whom reference is made and not the British people. In Christ, ev Xristos, *all* the nations of the earth will be blessed, and when He reigns (basileia) rules, He shall possess the "gate of the enemies"—*all* of His former enemies—for He shall be King of Kings and Lord of Lords and "have dominion from sea to sea and from river even unto the ends of the earth."

1 Chronicles 9:1-3

So all Israel were reckoned by genealogies: and, behold, they were written in the book of the kings of Israel and Judah, who were carried away to Babylon for their transgression.
Now the first inhabitants that dwelt in their possessions in their cities were; the Israelites, the priests, Levites, and the Nethinims.

And in Jerusalem dwelt of the children of Benjamin, and of the children of Ephraim, and Manasseh.

British-Israelites insist that only the tribes of Judah and Benjamin with the Levites returned to the land of Palestine, but it is evident from the Biblical record that a remnant from *all* the tribes returned. The evidence is found in these verses. In this passage of Scripture one will find not only the tribes of Judah and Benjamin, but Ephraim and Manasseh. It should be noted from no other extraneous material or outside sources brought in that verse 2 states that those returning were definitely Israelites—a term which Anglo-Israel writers *maintain* applies to the inhabitants of the Northern Kingdom.

Ezra 2:28

Now these are the children of the promise that went up out of the captivity, of those which had been carried away, whom Nebuchadnezzar the king of Babylon, and come again unto Jerusalem and Judah, every one unto his city. The men of Bethel and Ai, two-hundred and twenty-three.

We learn from this passage of Scripture that these men from two northern cities also returned with the remnant. In verse 59 of this same chapter, the question of genealogy is raised and the returning exiles are required to show that they are of Israel, not of Judah or Benjamin.

Isaiah 27:6 and 3:1-2

He shall cause them that come of Jacob to take root; Israel shall blossom and bud, and fill the face of the world with fruit (v. 6).

The wilderness and the solitary place shall be glad for them, and the desert shall rejoice, and blossom as the rose (v. 1).

It shall blossom abundantly, and rejoice even with joy and singing: the glory of Lebanon shall be given unto it, the excellency of Carmel and Sharon, they shall see the glory of the Lord, and the excellency of our God (v. 2).

Even though British-Israelites claim this promise is Great Britain, those of us who deal with the original languages know that "In That Day" means a prophecy to be fulfilled. "In That Day," to any knowledgeable person of the Bible, this phrase refers to the millennial glory. If these people who have the "keys" to Bible interpretation would go to verse 12, they would see that "In That Day" would also see the fulfillment of "And ye shall be gathered one by one, O ye children of Israel."

Strangely enough, British-Israelites or Armstrongites ignore this verse because they know that it does not apply to the British nation; for when were they ever gathered one by one? These passages are only true of Israel, as the Scriptures make clear.

Deuteronomy 8:18, 28:12

But thou shalt remember the Lord thy God; for it is he that giveth thee power to get wealth, that he may establish his covenant which he swore unto thy fathers, as it is this day.

The Lord shall open unto thee his good treasure, the heaven to give the rain unto thy land in his season, and to bless all the work of thine hand: and thou shalt lend unto many nations, and thou shalt not borrow.

To be able to come out with Great Britain from these verses is the poorest excuse for Biblical exegesis, but people are falling for this kind of Bible interpretation. There is no other nation under God's creation but Israel in the land that this passage is talking about.

To be more technical and even more embarrassing and "borrowing from none," we could mention England's War Debts.

This writer does not want *only* a careful reading of the text, but a scholarly Bible exegesis of God's Word.

Daniel 2:45

Inasmuch as thou sawest that from this mountain
a stone was cut out without hands and crushed
the iron, bronze, clay, silver and gold, the great
God hath made known to the king what will be
after this; and sure is the dream and faithful its
interpretation.

The Jewish leaders of Christ's day called Him a blasphemer when He said, "I and my Father are one" (John 10:30). What are we to call Anglo-Israelism when they claim to be the stone in this passage?

The Hebrew word for stone used in this passage of Scripture is (אֶבֶן), meaning "the stone filled the whole earth." This stone is Christ. The stone is Messianically interpreted even in the Targum. Even in Rabbinic literature there are many instances of the reference of the stone to the Messiah. As a former Orthodox Jew, the writer resents the interpretation of British-Israelites in taking the place of Israel. This stone was prepared, not by man, but by God. "Jesus Christ Himself being the chief corner stone" (Eph. 2:20) (ἀκρογωνιαίον) in the Greek, speaks of Jesus as the key stone. "Wherefore also it is contained in the Scriptures, Behold I lay in Zion a chief corner stone, elect, precious, and he that believeth on Him (a Person) shall not be confounded" (1 Peter 2:6).

In this passage the Greek word (λίθος) speaks of Christ the *Stone* for *Salvation* and *Perdition*. Again and again we cannot mistake this word for anyone but Christ.

2 Kings 17:18-23

This passage of Scripture is frequently used by those who teach that the ten tribes are lost, especially verse 18 that will be dealt with. "Therefore the Lord was very angry with Israel, and removed them out of his sight: There was none left but the tribe of Judah only."

The words, "out of his sight," are said to indicate that the ten northern tribes disappeared into oblivion. The words, "there was none left but the tribe of Judah only," are used to show that only the descendants of this tribe are in existence today.

Let us be practical, but honest, as we examine the Scriptures more closely. The special place where Yahweh God dealt with His chosen people was the land of Palestine. The temple was there as the center of worship. Those who walked in obedience were allowed to live in the land, but when they disobeyed, they were taken from the land. Notice verse 18, "out of his sight," *means* only that the ten tribes were driven from the land. "There was none left but the tribe of Judah only." Left where? Left in the world? No! Left in the land of Palestine. There is no mystery that the ten tribes continued to exist after they were driven away from Palestine, which is beautifully brought out in verse 23, "They had not ceased to exist, they were only relocated in Assyria" (not Great Britain).

ARMSTRONG'S TEACHINGS ON
THE DOCTRINE OF THE CHURCH

Trinity

The historic position of Evangelicals and Fundamentalists that there is one God, existing in three persons—Father, Son and Holy Spirit, are not accepted by Armstrongism.

Armstrongism denies the personality of the Holy Spirit. Although its publications capitalize the name, the pronoun used is "it," since the Spirit is considered to be an impersonal force.

The Bible teaches from Genesis to Revelation that God is one, although existing in three persons. He is Triune. The use of the plural Hebrew noun, Elohim (אֱלֹהִים) translated "God" (Gen. 1:1), as well as the plural pronouns in Genesis 1:26 and 3:22, imply the different persons of the Godhead.

The Scriptures give clear evidence over and over again that the Holy Spirit is a person, not an impersonal force. The Holy Spirit has intellect (1 Cor. 2:10), emotions (Eph. 4:30), and will (I Cor. 12:11). If, as Armstrong says, the Holy Spirit is impersonal, why does the Holy Spirit, according to the Bible, have these characteristics?

He teaches (John 14:26), intercedes (Rom. 8:26), calls (Acts 13:2), directs (16:6-7), and empowers (Rom. 15:19).

How anyone or group can claim the Bible as their only authority and yet not present the PLAIN TRUTH about the Father, Son and Holy Spirit is beyond this writer.

Salvation

All the literature coming off the press at Ambassador College emphasizes that salvation is by faith, yet when you study their tenets, one finds that it is not by faith alone. Armstrongism brings back to this writer a legalistic system that kept him in bondage to works for many years.

The Philippian jailer asked what he needed to do to be saved and Paul answered, "Believe on the Lord Jesus Christ and thou shalt be saved" (Acts 16:31). Salvation throughout the Old and New Testament has always been by faith. Salvation itself is by grace through faith (Eph. 2:8-9).

There is too much mystery to Armstrong's teaching on salvation. His philosophy about this most important subject is not really certain until death. The Bible says the Holy Spirit lives within you when you trust Christ as your personal Savior (Rom. 8:9; Eph. 1:13). Ephesians 4:30 says, "ye are sealed unto the day of redemption." What do we do if we sin? "If we confess our sins he is faithful and just to forgive us our sins, and to cleanse us from all unrighteousness" (1 John 1:9).

The Christian life would be uncertain if it is not known until the time of death whether or not a person has eternal life. Yet, 1 John 5:13 says, "These things have I written unto you that believe on the name of the Son of God, that ye may know that ye have eternal life."

The writer has gone into a lengthy discussion on the Sabbath in a previous chapter. Therefore, there will be no need to dwell on this Seventh-day worship *MUST* or requirement for salvation. Scripture is the highlight of this section, therefore, Colossians 2:16 says to present day believers, "Let no man therefore judge you in meat, or in drink, or in respect of an holy day, or of the new moon, or of the sabbath days."

How Armstrong can twist the Word of God in John 3:7 to mean a physical resurrection instead of spiritual birth remains a mystery, and yet millions fall for these teachings. The term "born again," when Jesus is talking to Nicodemus, means "from above." "Unless you are born of the water and of the Spirit you cannot see the Kingdom of God."

One of the most important doctrines of the Christian Church is the doctrine of salvation. It is a sad state when poll after poll is taken and the results are tabulated with Christians not sure of their salvation. Men may differ on events of prophecy and church policy, but there is no middle ground. There is but one way of salvation!

Jesus when He was tempted by the devil used Scripture. "For it is written." There are many passages that one can use to refute those who claim salvation is by works. The writer would like to leave this section with four Scripture passages that will help the reader as he deals with confused people.

> *Verily, verily, I say unto you, He that hearest my word, and believeth on him that sent me hath everlasting life, and shall not come into condemnation, but is passed from death unto life (John 5:24).*

> *For by grace are ye saved through faith; and that not of yourselves; it is the gift of God (Eph. 2:8).*

> *Not by works of righteousness which we have done, but according to his mercy he saved us, by the washing of regeneration, and renewing of the Holy Spirit (Titus 3:5).*

> *He that hath the Son hath life; and he that hath not the Son of God hath not life. These things*

have I written unto you that believe on the name
of the Son of God; that ye may know that ye have
eternal life, and that ye may believe on the name
of the Son of God (1 John 5:12-13).

In connection with salvation, the Worldwide Church of God teaches that those who have died in this life without a chance to believe the gospel message will be resurrected at the close of Christ's one thousand year reign on earth and given an opportunity to believe. There is not a thread of evidence in Scripture to indicate there will be any future opportunity to accept Christ.

"Behold, now is the accepted time, behold, now is the day of salvation" (2 Cor. 6:2). And a note of finality: "It is appointed unto men once to die, but after this the judgment" (Heb. 9:27).

Heaven and Hell

How Armstrong can get away by denying the Biblical teaching of heaven and hell is a mystery, but seriously, his entire teaching is a mystery. The Bible clearly states, "I go to prepare a place for you. And if I go and prepare a place for you, I will come again, and receive you unto myself; that where I am, there ye may be also" (John 14:2-3).

Some passages on hell might set the record straight that the Bible talks about a real hell; everlasting fire (Matt. 25:41), eternal punishment (Matt. 25:46), everlasting destruction (2 Hes. 1:9). Heaven and hell are real places, according to Scripture.

SUMMARY

The refutations that have been made against every claim of British-Israelism have been done with prayer, research and documentation. The greatest source to refute statements made by any cult, sect or group is the Word of God. Scripture in its original languages have disproven tradition, theories, legends and prefabrications throughout all history.

This writer will take the stand Martin Luther took in the year 1521 when he said, on April 17th before the Emperor and Reichstag, "I cannot go against Holy Scripture. Here I stand. God help me."

The Biblical, Assyrian and archaeological record presented in this chapter is in agreement. The evidence from the Bible is of a remaining and continuing Israelite population. The nation at the beginning of the Intertestamental Period was a twelve-tribed nation. The localized ministry of Jesus was definitely to the "lost sheep of the house of Israel."

Every claim has been refuted with Holy Scripture and leading world exegetes.

ENDNOTES

[1]   George Leon Rose, *Real Israel and Anglo-Israelism* (Glendale: Rose, 1942), foreword.

[2]   James Strong, *Exhaustive Concordance of the Bible* (Nashville: Crusade, [n.d.]), p. 111.

[3]   David L. Cooper, *Messiah: His Nature and Person* (Los Angeles: Biblical Research Society, [n.d.]), p. 29.

[4]   David Baron, *Rays of Messianic Glory* (Grand Rapids: Zondervan, [n.d.~]), p. 258.

[5]   Richard W. DeHaan, *Israel and the Nations in Prophecy* (Grand Rapids: Zondervan, 1975), p. 58.

[6]   Canon Adam Fox, *The Pictorial History of Westminster Abbey* (London: Pitkin Ltd., 1969), p. 13.

[7]   Howard B. Rand, *The Covenant People* (Merrimac: Destiny, 1972), p. 59.

[8]   Richard Marson, *The Marson Report* (Seattle: Ashley-Calvin, 1975), p. 63.

[9]   Louis T. Talbot, *What's Wrong With Anglo-Israelism?* (Findley: Dunham, 1956), p. 30.

[10]   John F. Walvoord, *The Millennial Kingdom* (Findlay: Dunham, 1963), p. 197.

[11]   J. Dwight Pentecost, *Things to Come* (Grand Rapids: Dunham, 1964), p. 103.

[12]   J. J. Stewart Perowne, *The Book of Psalms, Vol. II* (Grand Rapids: Zondervan, 1966), p. 153.

[13]   David Baron, *The History of the Ten "Lost" Tribes: Anglo-Israelism Examined,* (London: Morgan & Scott, 1915), p. 74.

[14]   Herbert W. Armstrong, *The United States and British Commonwealth in Prophecy,* (Pasadena: Ambassador, 1967), pp. 111-123.

[15]   DeHaan, p. 53.

[16]   Roy L. Aldrich, *Anglo-Israelism Refuted* (Detroit: Central, 1935), p. 7.

[17]   Charles W. Walkem, *Contradictions, Absurdities, Errors of the British-Israel Myth,* (Glendale: Church Press, 1948), pp. 14-15.

[18]   Talbot.

[19]   Leon Rosenberg, *British-Israelism, True or False* (Los Angeles: American European Bethel Mission, [n.d.]), p. 6.

20   Samuel P. Tregelles, *Gesenius' Hebrew Chaldee Lexicon to the Old Testament* (Grand Rapids: Eerdmans, 1971), p 40 .

21   J. Weingren, *A Practical Grammar for Classical Hebrew* (Oxford: Clarendon, 1959), p. 309.

22   Ernst Adolph Knoch, *Refuse the Refuse, Anglo-Israelism* (Los Angeles: L.A. Concordance, [n.d.]) , p. 23.

23   Lawrence Duff Forbes, *The Baleful Bubble of "British Israelism"* (Victoria: Biblical Research Society,), p. 32.

24   Forbes, pp. 32-33.

25   DeHaan, p. 56.

26   Talbot, p. 21.

27   Gerhard Kittel and Friedrich Gerhard, eds. *Theological Dictionary of the New Testament, Vol. III*, trans. Geoffrey W. Bromiley. Grand Rapids: Eerdmans, 1977, p. 357.

28 .   Kittel and Gerhard, pp. 359-360.

29   Baron, *History of the Ten Lost Tribes*, pp. 40-43.

30   Anton Darms, *The Delusion of British-Israelism* (New York: Loiveaux Bros., [n.d.]), p. 50.

31   Harry Gray, "Eschatology of the Millennial Cults" (Master's thesis, Dallas Theological Seminary, 1956), p. 60.

32   W. W. Orr, *Can the Jew Survive?* (Wheaton: Scripture, 1961), p. 3.

33   Armstrong, p. 35.

34   Adolph Ernst Knoch, *Refuse the Refuse, Anglo-Israelism (Los Angeles: Concordance, [n.d.]), pp. 14-15.*

35   Knoch, p. 16.

36   Talbot, p. 43.

37   Knoch, pp. 20-21.

38   Allen H. Godbey, *The Lost Tribes a Myth* (New York: KTAV, 1974), preface, p. xx xii.

39   D. Winton Thomas, *Documents from Old Testament Times* (New York: Harper, 1961), p. 60.

40   Thomas, p. 59.

[41]   Magen Broshi, "Part of Ten Lost Tribes Located," *Biblical Archeological Review* (September, 1975), p. 27.

[42]   Broshi, p. 32.

[43]   G. Ernest Wright, *Shechem, the Biography of a Biblical City* (New York: McGraw-Hill, 1965), p. 164.

[44]   Wright, p. 166.

[45]   J. W. Crowfoot, G. M. Crowfoot, and Kathleen Kenyon, *Israelite Pottery, the Objects from Samaria* (London: Palestine Exploration Fund, 1957); p. 98.

[46]   Armstrong, pp. 20-24.

[47]   Tregelles, p. 726.

[48]   Strong, p. 102.

[49]   Tregelles, p. 726.

[50]   Rosenberg, p. 15.

[51]   Tregelles, pp. 612-613.

[52]   Roger F. Campbell, *Herbert W. Armstrong and His Worldwide Church of God* (Ft. Washington: Christian Literature Crusade, 1975), p. 103.

[53]   Campbell, p. 58.

[54]   A. J. Polloch, *The British-Israel Theory* (London: Loiveaux, [n.d.]), p. 31.

[55]   Charles L. Feinberg, *The Sabbath and the Lord's Day* (Whittier: Emeth, 1957), pp. 13-14.

Chapter 5

The Dangers of British-Israelism

INTRODUCTION

As a Hebrew-Christian, this writer objects to British-Israelism, Anglo-Israelism, Armstrongism, or any otherism claiming to be the Ten Lost Tribes of Israel. Especially does this writer object to the Anglo-Saxon nations stating they are Israel. The writer also objects to untruths which have come forth from this movement and have captured so many innocent people with their unscriptural teachings. When 150 million people have already been engulfed in this philosophy, the time has come to be alarmed.

When this author speaks about the dangers of British-Israelism, the term must be broadened to Armstrongism. The teachings of the Worldwide Church of God, of whom Armstrong is the head, is diametrically opposed to evangelical Christianity.

From what has already been shared about the teachings of the Worldwide Church of God, it is quite evident that the movement propounds as plain truth what is not taught in the Holy Scriptures, also teachings which have not been the teaching of historic Christianity since the Day of Pentecost. However, the most serious rules of hermeneutics have been abrogated and they are the views of God and salvation. Any group that teaches errors concerning the Godhead and a system of salvation by works, contrary to Scripture, should be avoided by the one who accepts the Scriptures as final authority.

Danger of Another Gospel

The Anglo-Israel teaching is dangerous because it puts into first place a message, which, even if true, is not the first or primary message of the Bible. Orthodox Christians agree that the most important message of the Bible is personal salvation by faith in Jesus Christ. Anglo-Israel writers will agree that this is the primary message of the Bible, but they proceed to a practical denial by promoting all of their emphasis and energies into promoting what they call "the Kingdom message." Mr. Howard B. Rand, Secretary-General of the Anglo-Saxon Federation of America, has written a tract called *Personal Salvation and Kingdom Redemption,* in which he attempts to refute this charge. His refutation is accomplished by evading the issue. He answers those who say that personal salvation is the only thing that matters and the only thing needed. This is not the contention of the opponents of Anglo-Israelism. Of course there are other things that matter, and that are needed besides personal salvation, but our contention is that the first and most important teaching is personal salvation.[2]

Dangers of Legalism

Sorry to say, but the writer is back to legalism again. The position of the British-Israelist is that the laws of Moses, with the exception of the ordinances, were not abolished at the cross. If we would only return to the laws of Moses, we will be blessed nationally and personally in material and spiritual things. There will be no more poverty nor sickness. This certainly sounds like we are in heaven. "And God shall wipe away all tears from their eyes" (Rev. 7:17), and there shall be no more death, neither sorrow, nor crying, nor pain (Rev. 21:4).

To make the Anglo-Israel position clear regarding the law, a quote from Mr. Rand's tract, The Old and New Covenants, p. 3:

> *No, the law has not been set aside. To cite*
> *Paul's declaration to prove that we are not*
> *under the law, but under grace, that we are not*
> *in bondage to the law, but free through Christ*
> *Jesus, only shows ignorance of the facts. Paul is*
> *discussing law which was added, because of sin.*
> *What was the law that was added to the*
> *commandments, statutes and judgments of the*
> *Lord at Mt. Sinai? A schoolboy should be able to*
> *answer. It was the law of ordinances that was*
> *our schoolmaster to bring us to Christ. [The*
> *New Testament teaches that we are not to come*
> *under bondage to the law]³*

In the light of God's Word, let us see if this Scripture can be trusted. Paul says in Romans 7:6, "But now we are delivered from the law." What does Paul mean by the law? Anglo-Israelism says he meant only the ordinances, but the next verse Paul quotes from "the law" and he quotes one of the Ten Commandments. Here is where the Anglo-Israelism falls apart when they say Paul means one thing by "the law" in verse 6, and another thing by "the law" in verse 7, and that is bad exegesis.

To continue, the suggestion was made that the consistent Anglo-Israelite must keep Saturday, the Old Testament Sabbath, and stop eating pork chops. Mr. Rand made the following frank but fatal reply: "I confess to you that I have not eaten it [pork], and I do not know the taste of it from my youth upward, and God has blessed me with health."⁴ The writer eats almost no pork at all, not because he came out of Orthodox Judaism, but because it is not good for you, especially in hot weather, and frankly, sickness does take hold of this aging body. The legalism we see here is not only apparent but confessed.

Phariseeism or legalism, as this author lived for one-third of his life, is one of the most persistent and deadly heresies of the church and the severest language of Scripture is used in its denunciation: "But though we or an angel from heaven, preach any other gospel unto you than that which we have preached unto you, let him be accursed" (Gal. 1:8).

Danger of Deceit

Every work that is examined in British-Israelism is deceitful. The Scriptures allude to those who handle the Word of God deceitfully. Mr. David Baron, outstanding Hebrew-Christian scholar, in his book on the Anglo-Israel question, gives this advice:

> *When reading Anglo-Israel literature, always verify your reference and study the context and you will find that the Scriptures quoted in them are either misapplications or perversions of the true meaning of the text.*[5]

Here are a couple of examples: In an Anglo-Israelite tract called *How We May* Locate Israel, by Fahy H. Jackson, on p. 6 we read:

> *From reference to 1 Chron. 5:17 we know that Dan, as a tribe, had left the land and was, according to Deborah's statement in Judges 5:17, abiding in ships, plying these ships in the trade route of Tarshish, which route was well established when Jonah preferred sailing to Tarshish to handling a revival in Ninevah.*

Let us really read 1 Chron. 5:17. "All these were reckoned by genealogists in the days of Jothan, King of Judah, and in the days of Jeroboam, King of Israel."

The second passage quoted contains a question which is part of a poem, the song of Deborah: "Why did Dan remain in ships?"

Nowhere in these passages is there any proof that Dan as a tribe had left the land, but this tract would lead people to believe that his speculation about the tribe of Dan was based on Scripture.

Mr. Allen's book, *Judah's Sceptre and Joseph*'s *Birthright*, shows a map in the front of the book displaying Europe and the Near East, and with a line drawn northwest from Jerusalem to the British Isles.[6] Underneath the map is the quote from Isaiah 49:12-20, but if one looks closely enough, one will find the last part of verse 12 has been omitted, with no indication of this by the author (see Appendix J).

Danger of Prediction

"No man knoweth the hour or the day when Christ will return, only His Heavenly Father." Yet the Anglo-Israelism literature is saturated with prophecy. Mr. W. C. McKendrick, in his book, *The Destiny of the British Empire and the U.S.A.,* predicts that the battle of Armageddon and other earth-shaking events will take place in the years 1928-1934.[7] At this point there is no need for me to even comment on this absurdity.

RACIAL PREJUDICE AND ANTI-SEMITISM

Racism

While British-Israelism is untrue, it is not without peril. One of its most persistent dangers is the ease with which it justifies and fosters racial pride and prejudice.

The supposed supremacy of the Anglo-Saxon race is used as further proof that they are the lost ten tribes—a chosen people. A rather horrible example of this racism is found in W. A. Redding's book, *The Millennial Kingdom*:

> *I shall therefore take a shorter route through the subject by calling your attention to some facts, as they exist, which will convince you, without history, that the Anglo-Saxons are the Lost Ten Tribes of Israel.*

> *Go over the earth and collect together all the*
> *Anglo-Saxon people and put them in a bunch to*
> *themselves; then collect together all the other*
> *races of people, such as the Chinese, Japanese,*
> *Egyptians, Hindus, Malayas, Negroes, Indians,*
> *Arabians and many other kinds of human beings,*
> *and put them all together in a bunch to*
> *themselves. Then compare the one congregation*
> *with the other. In the Anglo-Saxon bunch you*
> *will see high foreheads, long, slim intellectual*
> *noses, brilliant eyes, fine texture of the skin,*
> *well-proportioned physical frames and fine,*
> *smooth hair. Turn to the other group of races.*
> *There you will see the low, flat foreheads, heavy,*
> *short, thick noses, vicious eyes, coarse hair,*
> *and uncomely features.* [8]

Anti-Semitism

Along these same lines British-Israelism has sometimes led to, or has been used as justification for, anti-semitism. Normally it is the relatively mild form of blaming the Jews for the crucifixion of Christ, who thereby forfeited blessing and incurred cursing. Occasionally anti-Semitism becomes quite blatant, as in the book by Worth Smith, *The House of Glory*:

> *The Jews are still a part of the major House of*
> *Glory, altho of the separate House of Judah*
> *also. Be it carefully and distinctly noted here,*
> *however, that there are two kinds of Jews in the*
> *world today. One of them is the Sephardim Jew,*
> *who is of the ancient and eminent stock of old;*
> *the other is the Ashkenazim Jew, who is Jewish*
> *by religion only but who has very little, if indeed*
> *any at all, of the blood or talents of ancient*

Judah. It is this Ashkenazim Jew, and he alone,
who has spawned Communism and the other
deplorable features of the Anti-Christ and who
has foisted them on an undiscerning world to its
great detriment. The Ashkenazim is vastly
inferior to the Sephardim Jew, to whom he is no
blood relation in most cases, inferior in stock,
mentality, spirituality and works.[9]

The worst anti-Semitism, though, is to be found in Mr. Redding's previously cited *Millennial Kingdom:*

God designated one part as Israel and the other
part as Judah, and this part called Judah are the
Jews we see on our streets today, and we can
pick them out by their looks, as the Bible tells us
that God marked their faces so we can tell them
anywhere so that they can be persecuted for
killing Christ.[10]

Though it is easy to laugh at this belief system, one must never forget that a very ugly and a very dangerous thing can grow from this philosophy. British-Israelism often appeals to those who wish some justification for their racial prejudice, and when it comes to prejudice, facts do not seem to matter at all.[11]

WHAT ARE SATAN'S OBJECTIVES?

1. British-Israelism fosters foment, not felicity. British-Israelism destroys the peace of Christian congregations. From much experience, Pastor C. E. Palmer, of London, says, "When the British-Israelism comes in at one door, peace and harmony, with their correlative expressions, concerted and consecrated fellowship and service, go out by the other."

2. British-Israelism fosters feud, not fusion. British-Israelism divides the Christian communities. The reports of splitting of churches, both local and denominational, are multiplying. My own knowledge of this extends throughout Australia and New Zealand, and this author has received a recent report from South Africa to the same effect. Of this feature one friend writes, "It has caused our church a lot of sorrow throughout Australia. The whole thing is a trick of Satan to keep the people of God divided."

3. British-Israelism fosters futility, not fruit. British-Israelism dissipates the precious time of Christians by beguiling them into disputations pro and con on their philosophy. The Christian is a steward of the time entrusted to him by God. This author knows of nothing more calculated to frustrate the Christian "redeeming the time" than this mirage.

4. British-Israelism fosters fable, not fact. British-Israelism diverts the thoughts and activities of Christians from meditation upon the proclamation of the glorious Gospel of Christ. It is true that some addicted to the delusion do preach the Gospel, but it is emphatically equally true that generally considerably more energy and zeal and money are devoted to the untruth that "Britain is Israel" rather than to the truth that "Jesus is Christ."

5. British-Israelism fosters fulmination, not friendship. British-Israelism disseminates anti-Semitism. The anti-Jewish attitude of this false teaching is notorious. Lamentably, it is more observed by the Jewish people than by unsuspecting Christians. The anti-Semitism of British-Israelism is so pronounced that it has gained a mention in the Jewish Encyclopedia: "The Anglo-Israelite theory has of recent years been connected with the persecution of the Jews...."[12]

The Marson Report

Mr. Marson warns his readers not to fall for the convincing arguments put forth in this book. He pleads, "Do not make the mistake I made ten years ago when I accepted this theory without proving it. I accepted it and felt it was correct. But, I did not prove it."[13]

Continuing this discussion of misinterpretations of Scriptures, Mr. Marson shares this reflection on more than ten years of his life invested in following Armstrong:

> *Were it not a great tragedy, some of Mr.*
> *Armstrong's misinterpretations would seem*
> *quite funny. I guess many have laughed at them.*
> *The seriousness of the situation is brought home*
> *to me, however, when I realize that he fooled me*
> *for ten years. Today he has about sixty thousand*
> *of his members fooled.*[14]

CULTS: WHAT'S THE ATTRACTION?

What is a Cult?

Dr. Donald Metz, Assistant Professor of Sociology at Marquette University in Milwaukee, writes in Your Church magazine an indepth article on cults.[15] What is a cult? It is imperative to have some understanding as to what a cult is before we can attack the problem before us in this dissertation.

1. To begin with, cults are groups of people that reject traditional religious patterns. These people are usually alienated in some way from the majority of religious groups. They claim a new revelation or insight (Armstrongism).

2. Cults are usually built around a charismatic leader (Armstrong). Dare this writer mention Rev. Jim Jones of People's Temple.

3. The emphasis within the cult is on the individual, personal consensus rather than group concerns. Frequently attention is given to a search for mystical experience. The personal consensus seems to be expressed in two areas: (1) a search for identity, and (b) a search for direction.[16]

One could ignore this cult as a harmless group of fanatics if it were not for the fact that already an estimated 150 million people have embraced their teachings, and they are invading Protestant churches everywhere and leading children of God—particularly those of British descent—along dark labyrinths of twisted, heretical thinking. Not only have they violated every accepted rule of geography, history, philology, physiology and ethnology with their fables and their fancies, but they have "wrongly divided" the Word of truth and broken every rule of hermeneutics by their translation of God's Word.

It is our responsibility as teachers of the Word to warn men and women not to give heed to these "cunningly devised fables," but to search the Scriptures and to bring these doctrines under the lens of the Holy Writ.[17]

We are certainly in the last days. Cults and sects which bodily attack the fundamental doctrines of the Christian faith are flourishing on every hand, leading multitudes away from God. Together with these, there are vagaries that are being projected in order to destroy the testimony of those among God's people who are untaught in the sacred Scriptures. This writer calls upon the reader to exercise care about accepting any system of teaching until it has been placed under the lens of Holy Writ. Christian Science cannot stand when it is submitted to such a test; neither can Anglo-Israelism. If the reader accepts this theory, he repudiates the clear teachings of God's Word.

Influence of Other Religious Groups

The influence of other religious groups is quoted from the synopsis of Professor Paul Benware's doctrinal dissertation.

> *Herbert Armstrong strongly denies any indebtedness to the religious concepts, ideas or interpretations of other men. He claims that new truth, embedded in the Bible, has been revealed to him. However, it is the conviction of all outside the Worldwide Church of God, who have studied its system, that it is eclectic. Religious systems which were in existence before*

the Worldwide Church of God came on the
religious scene have had some of their teachings
incorporated into Armstrongism.

Seventh-day Adventism

The influence of Seventh-day Adventism through
the Church of God (Stanberry, Missouri)—an
offshoot of Adventism—is readily apparent.
Their positions on the place and importance of
the Sabbath, the keeping of the Law, the nature
and destiny of man and the new birth are nearly
identical. Other parallels can be observed in
teachings on the human nature of Christ, the
atonement of Christ, the definition of sin,
individual eschatology and the abstinence from
certain foods.

The Jehovah's Witnesses

Charles T. Russell, founder of this group, lived
and wrote long before the theology of the
Worldwide Church of God was formulated.
Both groups believe that the Trinity is a pagan
concept, the Holy Spirit is merely a force, the
resurrection body is spiritual, the wicked are
annihilated, and there is an opportunity for
salvation after death.

Mormonism

There are some strikingly similar teachings with
those of the Mormon Church. Especially
noteworthy are the teachings that deity is the

ultimate goal of man and that God planned the
fall of man.

The Church of God (Stanberry, Missouri)

Herbert W. Armstrong severed his relationship
with this group but evidently brought several of
its unique teachings along with him. Common to
both are such teachings as the importance of the
name "Church of God," the view of a Wednesday
crucifixion with a Saturday resurrection, and
severe condemnation of most holidays as
products of paganism.[18]

SUMMARY

The writer concludes this section with the following quote:

We must see the terrible danger in Anglo-
Israelism, not only in its substitution of a
counterfeit Messiah, not only in its denial of
God's purposes for Israel, not only in its
questioning of the promises of God and the
substitution of a worldly British empire for the
kingdom of God on earth, but also because the
whole system substitutes confidence in the flesh
for faith in the Lord Jesus Christ. Anglo-
Israelism is "another gospel" (2 Cor. 11:4). St.
Paul knew that he belonged to the children of
Israel. He was of that stock of the tribes, a
Hebrew of the Hebrews (Phil. 3:3-8). Confidence
in his family tree, confidence in his association
with Israel by his ancestry, he counted as dung

> *that he might win Christ. Anglo-Israelites go to*
> *this dung-heap, pick up its morsels and make it*
> *their only gospel. The fact that Paul belonged to*
> *the tribes and was able to trace his ancestry*
> *back to Adam counted him nothing. Any*
> *confidence in the flesh, any claim to racial*
> *superiority is only a detriment to the individual*
> *if he trusts in it instead of trusting in Christ. In*
> *the same chapter Paul tells us that those who*
> *mind earthly things, and certainly this is a*
> *description of Anglo-Israelism, are "enemies of*
> *the cross of Christ" (Phil. 3:18).*[19]

When a cult, sect or any group is obligated to refer to the Apocrypha for proof of its position, it must be hard-pressed for source material on which to prove its claims.

The saddest commentary of this movement is the deliberate unorthodox attempt on the part of some of its teachers to remodel and make over the Word of God to prove their contentions. When a movement destroys two of the greatest doctrines of the Christian Church, the Doctrine of God and Salvation, it is time to call this movement dangerous.

This chapter presents the terrible dangers in Anglo-Israelism with the summation of the following points:

1. Substitution of a counterfeit Messiah.

2. The denial of God's purposes for Israel.

3. The questioning of the promises of God.

4. Substitution of a worldly British Empire for the kingdom of God on earth.

5. Confidence in the flesh (works) for faith in the Lord Jesus Christ.

The writer would like to summarize this chapter with the following passages of Scripture:

> *That we henceforth be no more children, tossed*
> *to and fro, and carried about with every wind of*

doctrine, by the slight of men, and cunning
craftiness, whereby they be in wait to deceive;
but speaking the truth in love, may grow up into
him in all things, which is the head, even Christ
(Eph. 4:14-15).

Be not carried about with divers and strange
doctrines. For it is a good thing that the heart be
established with grace, not with meats, which
have not profited them that have been occupied
therein (Heb. 13:9).

ENDNOTES

[1]   Harold J. Berry, *Armstrongism, Is It the Plain Truth?* (Lincoln: Back to the Bible, 1974,) p. 24.

[2]   Roy L. Aldrich, *Anglo-Israelism Refuted* (Detroit: Central, 1935), pp. 2-3.

[3]   Aldrich, p. 4.

[4]   Aldrich, p. 5.

[5]   David Baron, *Anglo-Israel Examined* (London: Morgan and Scott, 1952), p. 51.

[6]   J.A. Allen, *Judah's Sceptre and Joseph's Birthright* (Merrimac: Destiny, 1917).

[7]   W.C. McKendrick, *The Destiny of the British Empire and the U.S.A.* (Toronto: Commonwealth, 1928), p. 197.

[8]   William A. Redding, *The Millenial Kingdom, A Book of Surprises* (New York: Ernest Loomis, 1894), pp. 45-48.

[9]   Worth Smith, *The House of Glory* (New York: Wise, 1939), pp. 113-114.

[10]   Redding.

[11]   Walter Martin, *The Kingdom of the Cults* (Minneapolis: Bethany, 1977), p. 297.

[12]   L. W. G. Duff Forbes, *The Baleful Bubble of British-Israelism* (Australia: Biblical Research Society, 1961), pp. 13-14.

[13]   Richard Marson, *The Marson Report* (Seattle: Calvin Ashley, 1970), p. 23.

[14]   Marson, p. 83.

[15]   Donald L. Metz,"Cults: What's the Attraction," *Your Church,* November/ December, 1979, p. 34.

[16]   Metz, p. 34.

[17]   Louis T. Talbot, *What's Wrong With Anglo-Israelism?* (Findlay: Dunham, 1956), pp. 3-4.

[18]   Paul N. Benware,"An Analysis of the History and Teachings of the Worldwide Church of God" (Ph.D. dissertation, Grace Theological Seminary, 1973), p. 6.

[19]   Talbot, p. 47.

CHAPTER 6

THE VALUE OF THIS STUDY FOR EVANGELICAL PASTORS AND LAITY IN THE WESTERN PART OF THE UNITED STATES

INTRODUCTION

The world today is in a very precarious position. Everyone who is keeping abreast of the times sees the "Signs of the Times" all around us. Someone recently said, "It is two minutes to twelve." One could say that the world is probably approaching the crossroads of history. According to educators, statesmen and scientists, the coming three years may prove to be one of the crucial periods of history.

The Theory Stated

Pastors as well as the laity from evangelical churches must know what British-Israelism believes before they can attack the problem.

Very briefly, the Anglo-Israel position is that the Anglo-Saxon peoples, especially Great Britain and the United States, are descended from the tribes of Israel of the Northern Kingdom, and therefore inherit the promises of Scripture. *The National Message*, the official journal of the British-Israel World Federation, introduces its articles with these words:

> *The following should be read in the light of*
> *Israel Truth—namely, that the Anglo-Saxon*
> *nations are the continuation of the Israel nation,*
> *the inheritors of her Charter; the possessors of*
> *her guarantees and immunities from destruction,*
> *the executors of her commissions.[1] (See*
> *Appendix A)*

As a Reference Book

A reference book, as generally understood, is a book to be consulted for some definite information rather than for consecutive reading.

In this dissertation the facts are usually brought together from a vast number of sources and arranged for convenient and rapid use in the footnotes and bibliography with additional supportive information in the appendix.

The Table of Contents makes the material covered in this dissertation readily accessible.

Great Britain Makes No Claims

To inform the Evangelical Community that neither the British government, nor the British nation, nor the Church of England make any claims as to Great Britain's being Israel. This teaching is solely the product of a movement within the Anglo-Saxon nation known as *British-Israelism.*

Discernment

To learn how to discern right from wrong, to be able to sift through the garbage that comes out of this movement takes insight from above. For example, *The Messenger of the Covenant*, official publication of the Anglo-

Saxon Federation of America, for September, 1933, states, "The object of the Anglo-Saxon Federation is to declare the gospel of the kingdom to our people."[2]

The following is an extract from a tract, *What is Anglo-Israel Truth?* by Howard B. Rand. On p. 6 we read:

> *These things being so, the Israel message of the Bible is the Anglo-Saxon message of the Bible. It is a glorious message, and will win our nation back to God, and fit her in turn to win the other nations to Him. Learn that great message and preach it, for this is the purpose of God concerning you, to whom He has said, "ye are my witnesses saith the Lord."[3]*

This writer is positive that if Mr. Rand knew the hermeneutics of Bible interpretation, he would have known that our Lord and Savior, Jesus Christ, had something else in mind other than the Anglo-Saxon message when He said, "ye shall be my witnesses in Judea, Samaria and to the uttermost parts of the world" (Acts 1:8).

Are Jews Israelites?

To inform the world that it was the Jews, all twelve tribes, that gave the world a Jewish Messiah and not just Ten Lost Tribes—Britain. To remind Evangelical Christians of the debt they owe the Jew. The Bible says "salvation is of the Jew" (John 4:22).

The words "Jew" and "Israel" are used interchangeably in the Scriptures. Paul was a Jew, Israelite and Hebrew. Nowhere in Scripture do we find the word "Jew" only from the tribe of Judah, for Paul was from the tribe of Benjamin and still called a Jew.

For many years the writer thought that because his birth was from the tribe of Judah, he was a Jew and not an Israelite, and heaven was assured.

In the refutation on this subject, a great deal of material is presented to strengthen the value in this respect.

Law vs. Grace

To inform the reader that it is not a system of works that saves, but the Son of God, the Lord Jesus Christ. It is not the Sabbath, circumcision, baptism or anything we can do.

The Armstrong clan believes that baptism is essential to salvation. Armstrong says:

> Then once you have made up your mind to yield to God, and to become a member of His Church— not some denomination, WRITE TO US immediately, telling us that you want to be baptized this summer. Plans are already being laid for baptizing tours to cover the United States and other areas of the world.[4]

Meredith says in his book on *The Ten Commandments*:

> Jesus founded only one Church. You need to find out about this Church. Write immediately for the free booklet. This is the Worldwide Church of God. Our ministers are ready to tell you how to keep the Sabbath.[5]

Armstrongism is a system of law (legalism). The gospel is a system of grace. "For the law was given by Moses, but grace and truth came by Jesus Christ" (John 1:17).

Blind Belief

While doing research on this dissertation, the writer came across a tract by J. G. Modin called, *British-Israel, What Does It Mean?* The author declares that, "only one *race* today answers in every detail to Israel, and that is the English speaking race—the British Empire and the United States."

Pastors of Evangelical Churches *must* share with their congregations that they cannot believe everything they read. In the writer's search for truth, British-Israelism material seemed so wonderful on the surface, with beautifully done magazines, but when one did some examining, one found out the Scriptures were misquoted or part of a verse left out, or from some Apocryphal Book which isn't even acceptable as far as scholarship goes.

The Bible as the Only Text Book

The following words were taken from a book by Gladys Taylor: "It is sufficient to say that we can trace the Hebrew race by migration over land and sea, to western Europe and the British Isles."[6]

Nowhere in Scripture is there any reference at all for a migration of God's chosen, His Promised People, to go anywhere but to remain true to the Promise in Gen. 15:18.

Our faith should be in the Word of God, not in Mary Baker Eddy's book, The Book of Mormon, The Apocrypha, or Ellen White's Bible.

Indepth Bible Study

This study should point up to pastors of Evangelical Churches the desperate need for indepth, intense and intelligent Bible study. This should include a thorough and scholarly study of Biblical prophecy led by informed and trained teachers.

Each pastor, himself, should lead an elective course on cults at least once every two years, which should include a seminar on British-Israelism. Armstrongism for church leaders is a *must*.

Resources

For anyone doing a study on this subject or merely looking for information, this dissertation can be invaluable.

First of all, the reader will find out the originators of this movement. Second, what is British-Israelism?

Third, who are the leading proponents of this movement in the twentieth century? Fourth, what radio coverage do they have? Fifth, who are their publishing companies? Sixth, to realize that Armstrongism has its International Headquarters in Pasadena, California, Ambassador College. Mormonism has its World Headquarters in Salt Lake City, Utah; Seventh-day Adventists and Jehovah Witnesses are large in number on the West coast.

Correct Bible Exegesis

British-Israelites twist practically every Bible verse they use in their claims. Pastors must be alerted to this danger, especially those who do not know the original languages. Armstrongism does much *eisegesis* but little exegesis. The reason for this is that they want to fit Scripture into their beliefs.

To interpret Scripture properly, we must know the scientific method of interpretation, which is called hermeneutics. First of all, in the writer's exegesis of a certain passage of Scripture, the original language is a must. Since many pastors do not know the original languages, they must go to reliable grammars, lexicons, concordances, journals, Bible dictionaries and commentaries.[7]

A good axiom for Bible exegesis is that we may assert that nothing should be elicited from the text but what is yielded by the grammatical explication of the language.[8]

The writer would like to share with pastors John 1:1 to bring out the full meaning of this verse: "In the beginning *was* the Word."

Now it is very important to pay attention to grammatical details. Tense usually refers to location in time, or state or completion or of existence in time. In the passage before us we notice that *was* is in the imperfect tense. The imperfect tense implies a previous state and its continuance and this is how this verse should be translated: "In the beginning the Word had been *existing,* and is still existing."

Notice what this verse is really saying. He was already existing before the dawn of creation.[9]

Believing the Scriptures to be the Word of God, we *must* exercise all of our ability not to overlay it with our own thinking. In every case where human error enters, divine truth is obscured and this is so prevalent with Armstrongism.

Barrows wrote some words that are relevant at this point:

> *Foremost among the qualities that belong to the interpreter is a supreme regard for truth. He will need a constant and vivid apprehension of the sacredness of all truth, more especially of scriptural truth, which God has revealed for the sanctification and salvation of men. "Sanctify them through thy truth, thy word is truth." These words of the Saviour he will do well to ponder night and day, till they become a part of his spiritual life; and to remember always, that, if such be the divine origin and high office of scriptural truth, God will not hold guiltless any who tamper with it in the interest of preconceived human opinions, thus substituting the folly of man for the wisdom of God*[10]

Letters From a British-Israelite

To help pastors of Evangelical Churches to *know how* to deal with such a bizarre movement as British-Israelism, which is taking people away from the true Word of God, the writer would like to quote from letters received from a friend of thirty-five years standing, who was an evangelical Baptist, worked with the Jewish people in our denomination, became a Seventh-day Adventist, and now, to my amazement, embraces British-Israelism. In college he was a Phi Betta Kappa honoree.

*Now, that you have informed me as to the title of
your dissertation, I cannot hold back any longer
to tell you that I am a British-Israelite. I will
send you all the material you need at once, so
that you can learn as much as possible about the
British-Israel message.*

*After reading the first book, Judah's Sceptre,
Joseph's Birthright by J. H. Allen, I subscribed
to two magazines and bought about twenty-five
books, some from the National Message
Publishing Co., Ltd., in London, England and
some from the Destiny Publishers in Merrimac,
Mass. I've been buying books ever since and
I've found the message of those books to be true
and Christian and of infinite value. It has to do
with the past, present and future history of the
people of God as spelled out in every book in the
Bible and forecasts their final restoration, which
Paul said would be "like life from the dead."*

*Once you have really absorbed the message and
are at home in it, your ministry will then be
revitalized more than you would believe now.*

*We have been in the "Last Days" since the
resurrection of our Lord. Now we are deep
within the "Time of the End." The message of
British-Israel is the message for our time. It
makes the Bible relevant to our day and to our
people who are being destroyed for lack of
knowledge. It is the Gospel of the Kingdom.[11]*

Another letter written a month apart, from the same person.

I hope I am not inundating you with information or discouraging you from examining it. I am trying to show you that you have just touched upon a whole world of knowledge of which you can have known almost nothing. But if you are willing to examine it with honest and open minds as Mike must have examined Christianity before he became a Christian, it will so expand your understanding of the Bible prophecy, God, man, and God's plan for Israel and Judah in these end times that you will never see things the same way again as you did before. And you will realize that our Lord accomplished vastly more at the cross than to provide personal salvation for whoever would believe, however vital that is. He also redeemed Israel strewn about the world in her exile and from that time Israel began to be restored.[12]

This note was written by my friend on the front cover of *Judah's Sceptre and Joseph's Birthright*:

Dear Mike and Chic:

This is a copy of the book that introduced me to British-Israel. The author was a devout Christian and a Methodist Bishop. It seemed to me he was trying too hard but he showed me so much truth that I couldn't deny, that my feet were set firmly on this road forever. The evidence is Biblical and secular and found in every walk of life, a mountain of small pieces.

Your friend.[13]

Can you see now why this dissertation was written?

SUMMARY

In the Bibliography of over seventy-five sources, there is not one book that incorporates the vast coverage of the entire field of British-Israelism as this dissertation does. The values of this study are limitless. The writer has only touched on the values of this study for Evangelical Christianity in the twentieth century, and for pastors in the western part of the United States. I pray that Evangelicals will wake up, because this area is the seed bed of many movements like British-Israelism or Armstrongism. May God bless you as you receive direction from this writing.

ENDNOTES

1   *The National Message* (London: Covenant, September, 1980), p. 141.

2   *The Messenger of the Covenant* ([n.p.]: Anglo-Saxon Federation of America, 1928).

3   Howard B. Rand, *What is Anglo-Israel Truth?*, p. 6. (tract)

4   Herbert W. Armstrong, "Is Water Baptism Essential?" *The Plain Truth*, June, 1967, p. 14.

5   Roderick C. Meredith, *The Ten Commandments* (Pasadena: Ambassador, 1977), p. 37.

6   Gladys Taylor, *Our Neglected Heritage: The Early Church* (London: Covenant, 1969), p. 13.

7   Bernard Ramm, *Protestant Biblical Interpretation* (Boston: W.A. Wilde, 1956), p. 133.

8   Ramm, p. 134.

9   Ramm, p. 134.

10   Ramm, p. 268.

11   Based on personal correspondence between John Hutton, Portland Oregon, and the writer, December 10, 1980.

12   Personal correspondence, September 11, 1980.

13   Personal correspondence, September 24, 1980.

CHAPTER 7

CONCLUSION

In concluding the writing of this dissertation, the author would like to quote the words of St. Paul, which were written on this very theme:

> *For I am not willing for you to be ignorant of*
> *this secret, brethren, lest you should pass for*
> *prudent among yourselves, that Israel in part,*
> *has become calloused until the complement of*
> *the nations may be entering (Rom. 11:25).*

If Britain is Israel, then she is calloused. But, thank God, many of them are not calloused, but earnest believers in Christ and the Scriptures, and they do not wish to glory in the flesh, but in Christ and His cross.

The Deciding Question

Were the ten tribes of Israel in the land of Palestine during the earthly ministry of the Lord Jesus Christ, or were only Jews, members of the tribe of Judah, present at that time? The complete theory of British-Israelism stands or falls according to the answer to this most important question.

The writer has shown in preceding chapters that *all* of the *Jews* were present in the land of Palestine when our Lord was upon earth. Also noted that the tribes were referred to in the New Testament. As far as this writer is concerned, *all* the British-Israelism fable breaks down in the light of God's everlasting Word.

The key to this entire problem that exists, and which this writer has tried to give honest answers lies in properly dissecting the Word of truth. Passages which apply to Israel in the kingdom of God, the millenial reign (basaleia), when physical features and privileges will again be recognized, are *wrenched* from their contexts and "applied" to a people and a time and an administration where they are a misfit. It is like trying to put on a pair of size 9 shoes when you wear size 11. It cannot be done.

In the millennium it will be an advantage to be an Israelite, but today it would be a hindrance. It is important for us to realize that we do not "glory" in the flesh, but in Christ Jesus. "The pride of life is not of the Father, but is of the world" (1 John 2:16).

In spite of the many volumes written on the subject of British-Israelism, both men and women before Armstrong, Anglo-Israelism has failed to prove its basic premise. When one considers that of the 35,000 promises contained in the Old and New Testaments, over 30,000 were distinctly given to Israel and therefore belong to Israel as a nation, it is easy to see how some may have correspondence in the English world today.[1]

The words of David Baron are perhaps of value in his opinion of British-Israelism, of which Armstrong is the leading proponent in the world today. Baron concludes that not only does this theory anticipate the blessings of the millennium, but:

> *Then, finally, it not only robs the Jewish nation,*
> *the true Israel, of many problems in relation to*
> *their future by applying them to the British race*
> *in the present time, but it diverts attention from*
> *them as the people in whom is bound up the*
> *purpose of God in relation to the nations, and*

> *whose "receiving again" to the heart of God,*
> *after the long centuries of unbelief, will be as*
> *"life from the dead" to the whole world.*[2]

Much prayer and research has gone into this dissertation. May God be pleased to use this work for His glory to the deliverance of many who embrace these false teachings of British-Israelism, and for the nurture and admonition (instruction and training) of His people in the true character of Christianity.

ENDNOTES

1   Anton Darms, *The Delusion of British-Israelism, A Comprehensive Treatise* (New York: Loiveaux Bros, [n.d.]), p. 17.

2   David Baron, *The History of the Ten "Lost" Tribes: Anglo-Israelism Examined* (London: Morgan, 1952), pp. 52-53.

THE BRITISH ISRAEL WORLD FEDERATION

STATEMENT OF BELIEF

The following manifesto of our beliefs was adopted by the Covenant People's World Council at their Meeting held in London in 1965, and which was later confirmed by the respective organizations.

We believe that Jesus, the Messiah or the Christ, is, was, and always will be God the Son, the Second Person of the Holy Trinity, and that He took our human nature upon Him in order that He might become the Redeemer of His Servant Nation Israel, and the only Saviour of all mankind.

While acknowledging God the Son to be the Living Word, we believe that the Bible is the Word of God written. We believe that chosen men spoke therein as they were moved by God the Holy Spirit, and that the canonical books of

*the Old and New Testaments are the final
authority in all matters of faith and doctrine.*

*We believe that in the matter of personal
salvation there is no distinction of race, class of
condition. Israelite, Jew and Gentile are equally
dependent upon the saving grace of the Lord
Jesus.*

*We believe that the Creator's Law as codified by
God Himself through Moses, as confirmed by
Jesus in the Sermon on the Mount and elsewhere,
is the indispensable foundation for a truly
Christian civilization.*

*We believe that this Law consisted of
Commandments, Statutes, Judgments and
Ordinances, and that the Ordinances were
fulfilled, or perfected, by Jesus at His
Crucifixion.*

*We believe that the descendants of Abraham,
through Isaac and Israel, were established as a
Servant Nation and Kingdom, in order that they
might bring the world to the knowledge of God,
to demonstrate His Law, and to proclaim His
love for all mankind. We also believe that certain
privileges were vouchsafed for them, not because
of any favouritism, but solely as a necessary
equipment for the discharge of their tremendous
responsibility.*

*We believe that God has been faithful to His
promises, and has developed the descendants of*

Israel into a nation and company of nations, and a great people. We further believe that these descendants are now identical with the nations and peoples of the British Commonwealth and Empire, of the United States of America and of other kindred nations.

We believe that the true, racial Jews of the present day (as distinct from Gentile proselytes of the Jewish faith) are the descendants of a comparatively small portion of the tribes of Judah, Benjamin and Levi which returned to Palestine from the Babylonian captivity; and that they can be reunited with the rest of Israel only when they accept the Lord Jesus as their Saviour.

We believe that the Throne and dynasty of David has been established by Covenant for ever, and that they now exist in the Royal House of Britain. We also believe that the Returning Christ will occupy this Throne and reign, at first over Israel, but eventually, and through the loyal service of Israel, over the whole world.

We believe that the personal visible return of the Lord Jesus in power and great glory is part of God's great plan for the restoration of all Creation to a state of harmony with His gracious will.

We believe that it is our privilege and responsibility to proclaim the Teaching as set forth above and by so doing to prepare a truly

Christian community of Israel nations, eager to
fulfill their destiny and win the whole world for
the Everlasting King.[1]

ENDNOTE

[1]   BIWF, 6 Buckingham Gate, London, 1965.

STATEMENT OF ANGLO-ISRAELITE CREED

Some years ago, the magazine, *Biblical Truth For Bereans*, contained the following tenets of Anglo-Israelism, as stated by the "Anglo-Saxon Federation of America," in Haverhill, Mass.

> *1. The Bible does not state or infer that the Jews are God's chosen people. Judah and Israel are entirely distinct and separate entities. II Chronicle 11.*

> *2. The Bible made these prophecies and recorded these facts concerning Israel and the Jews. Israel was to find an island home and be moved no more. The Jews were to be strangers in all lands. Israel was to constitute a kingdom but the Jews were never to be a nation, until reunited with Israel. Jews were to remain under the law and Old Covenant, whereas Israel was to be a Christian people.*

3. Israel had nothing to do with the crucifixion of our Lord, not being in the land, except Benjamin, who accepted Him.

4. 'Ephraim' is England and 'Manasseh' represents the United States. Manasseh was the thirteenth tribe, and that accounts for the discovery of America on October 13, 1492; and the following 'thirteens' in American history: thirteen colonies; 13 bars and 13 stars (flag); 13 letters in 'E Pluribus Unum' and 13 features, 13 olives, and 13 arrows on American coins. First American navy, 13 ships, Cornerstone of White House laid October 13, 1792. The 13th amendment abolished slavery. General Pershing born September 13, 1860 and arrived in France for participation in the World War June 13, 1917. The first letter in Manasseh is the 13th born in England and Hebrew languages. Herbert Hoover and Charles Curtis each had 13 letters in their names.

5. The Celtic-Anglo-Saxons are Israel, the chosen people of God. The British Isle inhabitants are descendants among others, from the tribes of Saxons (Isaac's sons), the Danes of Dan, the Jutes of Judah, the Fresians, the Picts, and the Scots, and Normans of Benjamin.

6. 'Brith' in Hebrew means 'covenant'; therefore, we have Britain, 'covenant law', British the 'covenant man', Brittania 'covenant ships'. 'Brittania rules the waves', controlling the English Channel, Gibraltar, Singapore,

Shanghai, Hong Kong, the Suez Canal, Malta, Aden, and other gates and stations. America controls practically all of the remaining gates. This, all in fulfillment of Genesis 22:17, 'thy (Abraham's) seed shall possess the gate of his enemies' (read Isaiah 14:1 to 8).

The Anglo-Saxons are 'Christianized Israel' and are fulfilling Isaiah 49:7: 'I will also give thee for a light to the Gentiles, that thou mayest be my salvation unto the end of the earth.' The Church is the priesthood of the nation.

In 1776 A.D. the Lord divided Israel into two nations, so that God's promises to both Ephraim and Manasseh might be realized.

7. When General Allenby, the British soldier, drove the Turks out of Palestine and took possession of that land, the British were the children of Israel from the north and all lands returning to the land given to their fathers by God, in fulfillment of Jeremiah 23:7 and 8.

During the centuries before this return of Israel (the Anglo-Saxons) to Palestine, God has fulfilled Ezekiel 20:33 to 35, bringing scattered Israel with a mighty hand out of countries into the wilderness (Great Britain) and the wilderness was to blossom like a rose, and be the place prepared of God where Israel should be nourished. And there Israel was to fulfill Deuteronomy 32:13, and be the lion lifting himself up with the strength of the unicorn—as a great Lion. Numbers 23:24, 24:9.

8. In this latter day the New Covenant is first for the Anglo-Saxon Israelites. As under the Old Covenant, strangers and sojourners can become Israelites, members of the kingdom nation (Britain) and partaker of its benefits. These partakers are grafted into the Israel stock for kingdom benefits. Every Anglo-Saxon who complies with the law is recovenanted to God. The law has not been set aside, only the form of circumcision. The punishment of those refusing to comply with this law shall be destruction.

The present failure of Anglo-Saxons and Americans to recognize Great Britain as the kingdom of Israel is responsible for the present misery and suffering in the two lands. Israel's time of punishment foretold in Daniel 4:23 and 32 'seven times' has expired. 'Seven times' was a period of 360 weeks, or 2520 years. Adding 2520 years to the time of Judah's captivity, about 600 B.C., we come to about 1920 A.D. One of the chief speakers for the Anglo-Israelites declares the Lord will come for His Church September 16th, of the year (1936).

9. Only Spirit-filled Christians will be saved from the great time of trouble. The rest of the Church and all Israel (Britons) will survive until Jesus' feet stand on the mount of Olives to save His people from destruction, in fulfillment of Zechariah 14:1 to 3 (Howard B. Rand). The wise virgins of Matthew 25 are the Spirit-filled

Church members who will be raptured. These
will know in advance the arrival of the day of
their removal. This will include only a few.

10. (Rev. Wm. P. Goard). The throne of David
has come down to Great Britain through a clear
line of descent and therefore the fulfillment of
God's promise that David's throne would endure
forever. Great Britain and America, Ephraim
and Manasseh (who are to render willing
obedience) are preparing the way for the coming
of the King. The house of David, removed from
Jerusalem in the days of Nebuchadnezzar, was
brought to Ireland by Jeremiah the prophet in
the person of Tamar Tephi, thus establishing the
present line of descent. The Ten Tribes came
from Assyria to Europe, thence to the British
Isles to be joined to the house of David, God's
Jehovah throne was established in the midst of
His kingdom, Modern Israel, or Britain. An
ancient King of Ireland was married to a Jewish
Princess from the East and their coronation was
on Jacob's stone, and the royal house of Britain
descended from that union.

The present King of England, Edward Albert
Christian George Andrew Patrick David is the
prince descended from King David, the one
hundredth generation from King David born
1076 B.C. His name was at the suggestion of the
Marchioness of Waterford, for said she, 'I
believe he will be David your prince foretold by
the prophet, under whom we shall repossess the
holy land.' The royal mother replied, 'Baby is

*called David'. The present King David is on the
throne and Ezekiel 37:34 is fulfilled.*

*11. According to Daniel 2:44 and 45, a Stone is
to come from heaven, smite all other kingdoms,
become a mountain, and fill the whole earth.
This Stone kingdom is to stand forever, Israel is
to stand forever, Jeremiah 31:35,36. Therefore
Great Britain is the Stone Kingdom, the forever
Israel. To prove this, there are two emblematic
stones, the little stone in Britain's possession
and the big stone, the pyramid of Egypt. This
stone in Egypt is the altar of Isaiah 19:19 and
20, God's witness.*

*The little stone now occupies the chief seat in
the kingdom, the coronation chair at Westminster
Abbey. The Kings of the House of David have
been crowned upon this stone. During the past
130 years the Kingdom of Great Britain has
expanded into the mountain and the emblematic
big stone, the pyramid, is God's witness to Great
Britain's claim.*

*The Anglo-Israelites decide much by the
structure and measurements of the pyramid.
They say 'When the time arrived for the Kingdom
to grow into a mountain, God revealed a
mountain of stone as a witness to the Kingdom
people. Cutting the pyramid open from north to
south, the diagram of the passages gives a
chronological history of Israel and Judah'. There
is recorded that the transfer of the Kingdom
activities was from Judah to Israel, because the*

*Jews, and not Israel, crucified Christ. Even the
very time of Britain's ultimatum to Germany,
and the Anglo-Saxon's entrance into the World
War in 1914, is told of the pyramid
measurements, midnight August 4 that was the
beginning of Jacob's trouble in fulfillment
according to Jeremiah 30-7.*[1]

ENDNOTE

[1]   Anglo-Saxon Federation of America, Haverhill, Mass., 1928.

CANAAN AS DIVIDED AMONG THE TWELVE TRIBES

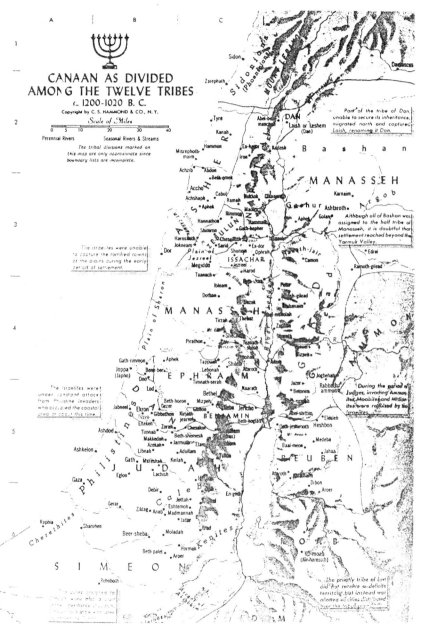

CANAAN AS DIVIDED
AMONG THE TWELVE TRIBES
c. 1200-1020 B. C.
Copyright by C. S. HAMMOND & CO., N. Y.

Scale of Miles

0   5   10   20   30   40

Perennial Rivers   Seasonal Rivers & Streams

The tribal divisions marked on
this map are only approximate since
boundary lists are incomplete.

THE KINGS OF ISRAEL

Name	Date of Reign	Relation to Predecessor	Years Reign	Char-acter	Manner of Death	1 Kings	2 Chronicles
Jeroboam	931-910		22	Bad	Stricken by God	11:26-14:20	9:29-13:22
Nadab	910-909	Son	22	Bad	Murdered by Baasha	15:25-28	
Baasha	909-886	none	24	Bad	Murdered by Zimri	15:27-6:7	16:1-6
Zimri	885	Captain of Chariots	7 days	Bad	Suicide	16:9-20	
Omri	885-874	Army Captain	12	Bad	Died	16:15-28	
Ahab	874-853	Son	22	Bad	Wounded in Battle	16:28-22:40	18:1-34
Ahaziah	853-852	Son	2	Bad	Fell through lattice	22:40-2 Kings 1:18	20:35-37
Jehoram*	852-841	Brother	12	Bad	Murdered by Jehu	2 Kings 3:1-9:25	22:5-7
Jehu	841-814	none	28	Bad	Died	9:1-10:36	22:7-12
Jehoahaz	814-798	Son	17	Bad	Died	13:1-9	
Jehosah**	798-782	Son	16	Bad	Died	13:10-14:16	25:17-24
Jeroboam II	793-753	Son	41	Bad	Died	14:23-29	
Zechariah	753-752	Son	6 mon.	Bad	Murdered by Shallum	14:29-15:12	
Shallum	752	none	1 mon.	Bad	Murdered by Menahem	15:10-15	
Menahem	752-742	none	10	Bad	Died	15:14-22	
Pekahiah	742-740	Son	2	Bad	Murdered by Pekah	15:22-26	
Pekah	752-731	Army Captain	20	Bad	Murdered by Hoshea	15:27-31	28:5-8
Hoshea	731-722	none	9	Bad	Deposed to Assyria	15:30-17:26	

THE KINGS OF JUDAH

Name	Date of Reign	Relation to Predecessor	Yrs. of Reign	Character	Manner of Death	1 Kings	2 Chronicles
Rehoboam	931-913	Son	17	Bad	Died	11:42-14:31	9:31-12:16
Abijam***	913-911	Son	3	Bad	Died	14:31-15:8	13:1-22
Asa	911-870	Son	41	Good	Died	15:8-24	14:1-16:14
Jehoshapat	873-843	Son	25	Died	Died	22:41-50	17:1-20:37
						2 Kings	
Jehoram	853-841	Son	8	Bad	Stricken by God	8:16-24	21:1-20
Ahaziah	841	Son	1	Bad	Murdered by Jehu	8:24-9:29	22:1-9
Athaliah	841-835	Mother	6	Bad	Murdered by Army	11:1-20	22:1-23:21
Joash	835-796	Grandson	40	Good	Murdered by Servants	11:1-12:21	22:10-24:27
Amaziah	796-767	Son	29	Good	Murdered	14:1-20	25:1-28
Azariah****	792-740	Son	52	Good	Stricken by God	15:1-7	26:1-23
Jotham	750-732	Son	16	Good	Died	15:32-38	27:1-9
Ahaz	735-716	Son	16	Bad	Died	16:1-20	28:1-27
Hezekiah	716-687	Son	29	Good	Died	18:1-20:21	29:1-32:33
Manasseh	697-643	Son	55	Bad	Died	21:1-18	33:1-20
Amon	643-641	Son	2	Bad	Murdered by Servants	21:19-26	33:21-25
Josiah	641-609	Son	31	Good	Wounded in Battle	22:1-23:30	34:1-35:27
Jehcahaz	609	Son	3 mon.	Bad	Deposed to Egypt	23:31-33	36:1-4
Jehoiakim	609-598	Brother	11	Bad	Died in Siege?	23:34-24:5	36:5-7
Jehoiachin	598-597	Son	3 mon.	Bad	Deposed to Babylon	24:6-16	36:8-10
Zedekiah	597-586	Uncle	11	Bad	Deposed to Babylon	24:17-25:30	6:11-21

Note: Dates of some reigns overlap due to co-regencies.

*Joram, **Joash, ***Abijah, ****Uzziah

THE KINGDOMS OF ISRAEL AND JUDAH

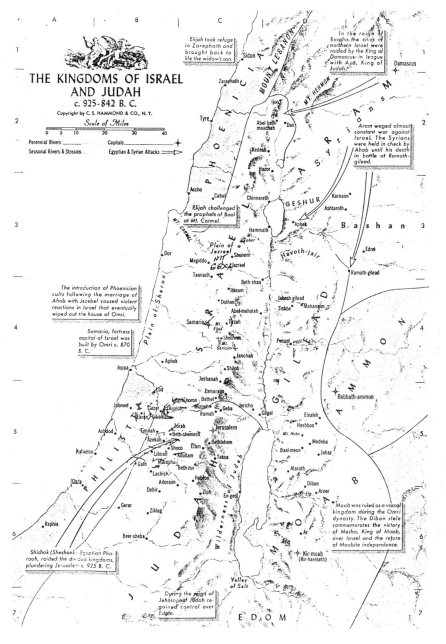

THE KINGDOMS OF ISRAEL AND JUDAH
c. 925-842 B. C.
Copyright by C. S. HAMMOND & CO., N.Y.

Scale of Miles

0   5   10   20   30   40

Perennial Rivers ─────   Capitals ─────

Seasonal Rivers & Streams ...   Egyptian & Syrian Attacks ⟹

Elijah took refuge in Zarephath and brought back to life the widow's son.

In the reign of Baasha the cities of northern Israel were raided by the King of Damascus in league with Asa, King of Judah.

Aram waged almost constant war against Israel. The Syrians were held in check by Ahab until his death in battle at Ramoth-gilead.

Elijah challenged the prophets of Baal at Mt. Carmel.

The introduction of Phoenician cults following the marriage of Ahab with Jezebel caused violent reactions in Israel that eventually wiped out the house of Omri.

Samaria, fortress capital of Israel was built by Omri c. 870 B.C.

Moab was ruled as a vassal kingdom during the Omri dynasty. The Dibon stele commemorates the victory of Mesha, King of Moab, over Israel and the return of Moabite independence.

Shishak (Sheshonk) Egyptian Pharaoh, raided the divided kingdoms, plundering Jerusalem c. 925 B.C.

During the reign of Jehoshophat Judah regained control over Edom.

JUDAH AFTER THE FALL OF ISRAEL

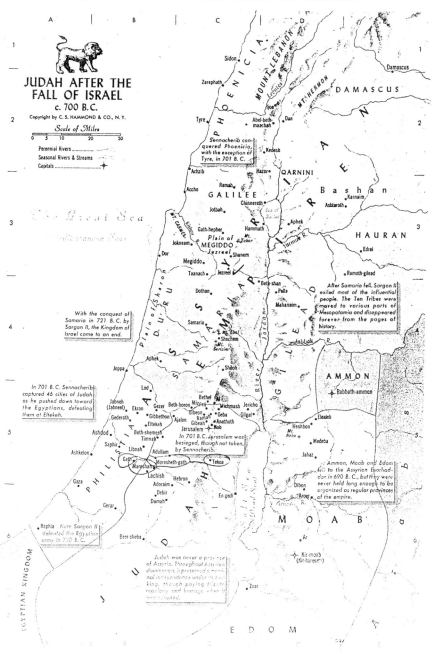

JUDAH AFTER THE
FALL OF ISRAEL
c. 700 B.C.

Copyright by C. S. HAMMOND & CO., N.Y.

Scale of Miles

0   5   10   20   30

Perennial Rivers ....
Seasonal Rivers & Streams ...-------
Capitals ....+

Sennacherib con-
quered Phoenicia,
with the exception of
Tyre, in 701 B.C.

With the conquest of
Samaria in 721 B.C. by
Sargon II, the Kingdom of
Israel come to an end.

After Samaria fell, Sargon II
exiled most of the influential
people. The Ten Tribes were
moved to various parts of
Mesopotamia and disappeared
forever from the pages of
history.

In 701 B.C. Sennacherib
captured 46 cities of Judah
as he pushed down toward
the Egyptians, defeating
them at Eltekeh.

In 701 B.C. Jerusalem was
besieged, though not taken,
by Sennacherib.

Ammon, Moab and Edom
fell to the Assyrian Esarhad-
don in 690 B.C., but they were
never held long enough to be
organized as regular provinces
of the empire.

Raphia here Sargon II
defeated the Egyptian
army in 720 B.C.

Judah was never a province
of Assyria. Throughout Assyrian
domination, it preserved a nomi-
nal independence under its own
king, though paying tribute
regularly and homage when it
was required.

THE ASSYRIAN EMPIRE

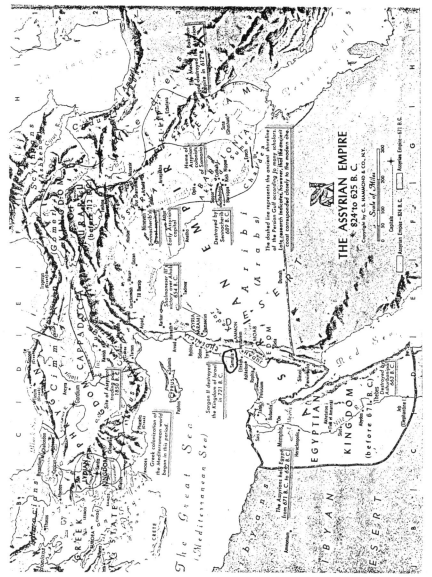

THE RESTORATION OF JUDAH

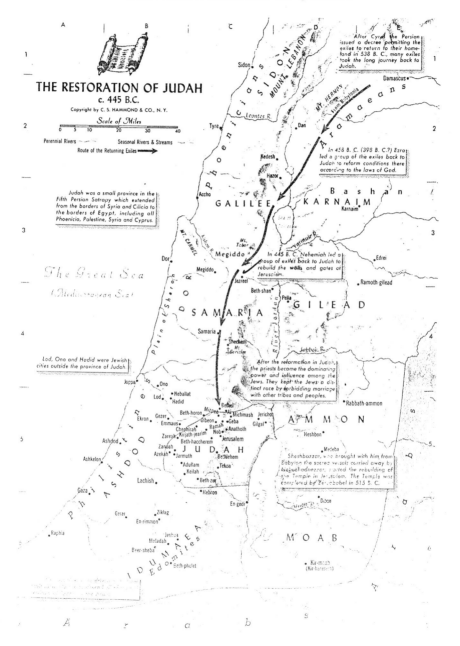

THE RESTORATION OF JUDAH
c. 445 B.C.

Copyright by C. S. HAMMOND & CO., N. Y.

Scale of Miles

0   5   10   20   30   40

Perennial Rivers ———   Seasonal Rivers & Streams ———
Route of the Returning Exiles ➡

After Cyrus the Persian issued a decree permitting the exiles to return to their homeland in 538 B. C., many exiles took the long journey back to Judah.

In 458 B. C. (398 B. C.?) Ezra led a group of the exiles back to Judah to reform conditions there according to the laws of God.

Judah was a small province in the Fifth Persian Satrapy which extended from the borders of Syria and Cilicia to the borders of Egypt, including all Phoenicia, Palestine, Syria and Cyprus.

In 445 B. C. Nehemiah led a group of exiles back to Judah to rebuild the walls and gates of Jerusalem.

After the reformation in Judah, the priests became the dominating power and influence among the Jews. They kept the Jews a distinct race by forbidding marriage with other tribes and peoples.

Lod, Ono and Hadid were Jewish cities outside the province of Judah.

Sheshbazzar, who brought with him from Babylon the sacred vessels carried away by Nebuchadnezzar, started the rebuilding of the Temple in Jerusalem. The Temple was completed by Zerubbabel in 515 B. C.

THE JOURNEY FROM ISRAEL TO THE BRITISH ISLES

"I am a father to Israel, and EPHRAIM is my first-born. * * Declare it in the isles afar off, and say, He that scattered Israel will gather him, and keep him, as a shepherd doth his flock." Jer. 31: 9, 10.

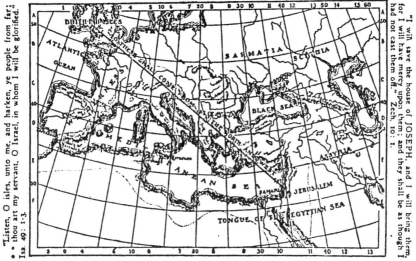

"Behold these (Israel in the isles) shall come from far, and lo, these from the north and from the west. The children which thou shalt have, *after thou hast lost the other*, shall say again in thine ears, The place is too strait (cramped) for me, give a place to me that I may dwell. Isa. 49: 12, 20.

EPHRAIM—ISRAEL IN THE ISLES.

HISTORICAL BASIS
FOR ANGLO-ISRAELISM WANTING

A letter was sent by the writer to several of our leading institutions of higher education, addressed to the Department of History. The letter contained this question: "Do you know of any historical evidence to support the theory that the Anglo-Saxon people are descended from the ten tribes of Israel? Here are the answers received:

> *So far as I am aware no reputable historical accepts the theories of the people known as the Anglo-Israelites. There is a considerable body of literature on this subject, largely originating in England, but none of it, I believe, contains much more than speculation on probabilities, plus Biblical interpretations of questionable soundness. Professional historians are agreed that the people who are now called Anglo-Saxon are a mixture of Teutonic, Norman French, and some Celtic blood. Any good, modern textbook, such as W. E. Lunt's History of England*

(Harper's), will give you this information. If the Anglo-Saxons are descended from the ten tribes, the Germans, Scandinavians, French, Scotch and Irish must be also. (from the University of Chicago)

As you doubtless know, there is a small group of English people who believe that they and all their fellow countrymen are descended from the "Ten Lost Tribes," but their assertion is based almost entirely upon their own peculiar interpretation of certain passages in the Bible, and has no smallest scrap of historical evidence to support it. (from Princeton University)

I beg you to state briefly that the last substantial publication on the Lost Ten Tribes is that of Professor Allen H. Godbey, entitled, **The Lost Tribes, a Myth**, *1930. There you will find an extensive bibliography on the subject. Incidentally the prevalent scholarly opinion shares Professor Godbey's view that the ten tribes have not left behind them sufficient historical records which allow us to trace them down to the more recent periods. (from Columbia University)*

I am aware that this theory has been mooted by a certain class of people for some time, and that an organization evidently well supplied with funds occasionally inserts full page propaganda articles in London newspapers in support of it. So far as I know, no reputable historian has ever taken it seriously. (from Michigan State College)

> *To the best of my knowledge no reputable historian has ever even entered the suggestion that there is any connection between the ten tribes of Israel and the Anglo-Saxons. The ten tribes, to the historian, were never "lost," except in the sense that they were absorbed into neighboring peoples of the near East. There is a wide gap in space and time between the Israelites and the earliest known Anglo-Saxons, and there are no existing records that even suggest that this gap can be filled. (from Wayne University, Detroit, Michigan)*

It may be objected that these professors have given prejudiced answers, but this is hardly possible when the question is strictly an historical one. However, we do not rest our case upon authorities, and so will proceed to show from an actual examination of both sacred and secular history, that the opinion of the Anglo-Saxon or Anglo-Israel theory expressed by these students of history is correct.[1]

ENDNOTE

1   Roy L. Aldrich, *Anglo-Israelism Refuted*, pp. 13-14.

BIBLIOGRAPHY

BOOKS

Aldersmith, H. *The Fullness of the Nations.* London: Marshall, 1898.

Aldrich, Roy L. *Anglo-Israelism Refuted.* Detroit: Central, 1935.

Allen. J. A. *Judah's Sceptre and Joseph's Birthright.* Merrimac: Destiny, 1917.

Armstrong, Herbert W. *The U.S. and British Commonwealth in Prophecy.* Pasadena: Ambassador, 1972.

_____. *The U.S. and British Commonwealth in Prophecy.* Pasadena: Ambassador, 1975.

Bagster, Samuel and Sons. *The Apocrypha.* London: Samuel Bagster, [n.d.].

Baron, David. *The History of the Ten "Lost" Tribes: Anglo-Israelism Examined.* London: Morgan and Scott, Ltd., 1915.

_____. *Rays of Messianic Glory.* Grand Rapids: Zondervan, [n.d.].

Berry, Harold J. *Armstrongism, Is It the Plain Truth?* Lincoln: Back to the Bible, 1974.

Cambell, Roger F. *Herbert W. Armstrong and His Worldwide Church of God.* Ft. Washington: Christian Literature Crusade, 1975.

Chambers, Roy R. *The Plain Truth About Armstrongism.* Grand Rapids: Baker, 1972.

Cooper, David. *Messiah: His Nature and Person.* Los Angeles: Biblical Research Society, [n.d.].

Crowfoot, J. W., G. M. Crowfoot and Kathleen Kenyon. *Israelite Pottery, The Objects From Samaria.* London: Palestine Exploration Fund, 1957.

Daines, Clem. *When Jesus Lived in Britain.* California: Clem Daines, [n.d.].

Darms, Anton, *The Delusion of British Israelism, A Comprehensive Treatise.* New York: Our Hope, [n.d.].

DeHaan, Richard. *British Israelism.* Grand Rapids: DeHaan, 1969.

_____. *Israel and the Nations in Prophecy.* Grand Rapids: Zondervan, 1975.

Dickey, C. R. *One Man's Destiny.* Merrimac: Destiny, 1951.

Epstein, Morris and Allen Howard Godbey. *The Lost Tribes a Myth.* New York: KTAU, 1930, Prolegomenon.

Feinberg, Charles L. *The Sabbath and the Lord's Day.* Whittier: Emeth, 1957.

Forbes, Lawrence Duff. *The Baleful Bubble of "British Israelism."* Australia: The Biblical Research Society.

Fox, Canon Adam. *The Pictorial History of Westminster Abbey.* London: Pitkin, Ltd., 1969.

Godbey, Allen H. *The Lost Tribes a Myth.* New York: KTAV, 1974.

Heath, Albon. *The Faith of a British Israelite.* London: Covenant, 1937.

Hine, Edward. *Identity of the Ten Lost Tribes of Israel with the Anglo-Celto-Saxons.* New York: Maranatha, [n.d.].

_____. *The British Nation Identified with Lost Israel.* London: S. W.

Partridge, 1964.

————. *The British Nation with the Lost Ten Tribes*. London: Partridge, [n.d.].

Jarrett, George F. *The Drama of the Lost Disciples*. London: Covenant, 1978.

Knoch, Ernst Adolph. *Refuse the Refuse, Anglo-Israelism*. Los Angeles: L.A. Concordance, [n.d.].

Lamb, W. *Anglo-Israelism and Israel*. New South Wales: Workers Trustees, 1935.

Marson, Richard. *The Marson Report*. Seattle: Ashley-Calvin, 1970.

Martin, Walter. *The Kingdom of the Cults*. Minneapolis: Bethany, 1966.

McKendrick, W. C. *The Destiny of the British Empire and the U.S.A.* Toronto: Commonwealth, 1928.

Meredith, Roderick C. *The Ten Commandments*. Pasadena: Ambassador, 1977.

Orr, W. W. *Can the Jew Survive?* Wheaton: Scripture Press, 1961.

Pentecost, J. Dwight. *Things to Come*. Grand Rapids: Dunham, 1964 .

Perowne, J. J. *The Book of Psalms*, Vol. II. Grand Rapids: Zondervan, 1966.

Polloch, A. J. *The British Israel Theory*. London: Loiveaux Bros., [n.d.].

Rambeston, J. H. *The Coronation Service*. Bedford: BIWF, [n.d.].

Ramm, Bernard. *Protestant Biblical Interpretation*. Boston: W. A. Wilde, 1956.

Rand, Howard B. *Anglo-Saxon Federation of America*. Haverhill: Destiny, 1928.

————. *The Covenant People*. Merrimac: Destiny, 1972.

Redding, William A. *The Millennial Kingdom A Book of Surprises*. New

York: Ernest Loomis, 1894.

Rose, George Leon. *Real Israel and Anglo-Israelism*. Glendale: Rose, 1942.

Rosenberg, Leon. *British-Israelism, True or False*. Los Angeles: American European Bethel Mission, [n.d.].

Smith, Worth. *The House of Glory*. New York: Wise, 1939.

Starkes, M. Thomas. *Confronting Popular Cults*. Nashville: Broadman, 1972.

Talbot, Louis T. *What's Wrong with Anglo-Israelism?* Findlay: Dunham, 1956.

Taylor, Gladys. *Our Neglected Heritage Division and Dispersion*. London: Covenant, 1974.

_____. *Our Neglected Heritage, The Early Church*. London: Covenant, 1969.

_____. *Our Neglected Heritage, The Magnet of the Isles*. London: Covenant, 1971.

Thomas, D. Winton. *Documents From Old Testament Times*. New York: Harper, 1961.

Walkem, Charles W. *Contradictions, Absurdities, Errors of the British-Israel Myth*. Los Angeles: Charles W. Walkem, 1948.

Walters, Charles W. *British Israelism Myth*. Los Angeles: [n.n.], 1948.

Walvoord, John F. *The Millennial Kingdom*. Findlay: Dunham, 1963 .

Weingren, J. A. *Practical Grammar for Classical Hebrew*. Oxford: Clarendon, 1959.

Wright, G. Ernest. *Schechem, the Biography of a Biblical City*. New York: McGraw-Hill, 1965.

PERIODICALS

Armstrong, Herbert W. "The World Wide Church." *The Plain Truth*, February, 1973, pp. 18-19.

_____. "Is Water Baptism Essential?" *The Plain Truth*, June, 1967, p. 14.

Fisher, Sir John Admiral. *The National Message*, 59, No. 1687, June-September, 1980.

Haggart, J. A. B. "Elizabeth—Monarch of Destiny." *Wake Up!*, July, 1980, p. 14.

McDaniel, F. Thomas. "National Consequences of Leaders' Choices. *Baptist Leader*, July 1, 1979, p. 19.

Metz, Donald L. "Cults, What's the Attraction?" *Your Church*, November-December, 1979, p. 34.

"We Believe." *New Vision*, April-June, 1969.

JOURNALS

Broshi, Magen. "Part of the Ten Lost Tribes Located." *Biblical Archaeological Review*, September, 1975, pp. 27, 32.

Nettelhorst, R. P. "British Israelism: A Miracle." *Biblical Research Monthly*, April-May, 1979, pp. 21-23; June, 1979, pp. 17-19.

The National Message [London], Vol. 59, No. 1688, July, 1980.

_____. Covenant, September, 1980.

DICTIONARIES, LEXICONS AND CONCORDANCES

Fr., H. "Tribes, the Twelve." *Encyclopedia Judaica*, Vol. XV, SUR-UN, E.J. Jerusalem: Keter, 1972.

Guralnik, David B. *Webster's New World Dictionary.* Prentice-Hall, Inc., 1976.

Hirsch, Emil G. "The Twelve Tribes." *Jewish Encyclopedia*, Vol. XII. New York: Funk & Wagnalls, 1916.

Jacobs, Joseph. "Lost Ten Tribes." *Jewish Encyclopedia*, Vol. XII. New York: Funk and Wagnalls, 1916.

Kittel, Gerhard and Friedrich Gerhard, eds. *Theological Dictionary of the New Testament*, Vol. III, trans. Geoffrey W. Bromiley. Grand Rapids: Eerdmans, 1977.

MacLean, A. B. "Rehoboam." *Interpreter's Dictionary of Bible.* New York: Abingdon Press, 1962.

Rabinowitz, Louis Isaac. "Ten Lost Tribes." *Encyclopedia Judaica*, Vol. XV. Jerusalem: Keter, 1971.

Strong, James. *Exhaustive Concordances of the Bible.* Nashville: Crusade, [n.d.].

Tregelles, Samuel P. *Gesenius' Hebrew-Chaldee Lexicon to the Old Testament.* Grand Rapids: Eerdmans. 1971.

Wigram, George V. and Ralph D. Winter. *The Word Study Concordance.* Wheaton: Tyndale, 1978.

UNPUBLISHED SOURCES

Benware, Paul N. "An Analysis of the History and Teachings of the Worldwide Church of God." Ph.D. dissertation, Grace Theological Seminary, 1973.

Gray, Harry. "Eschatology of the Millennial Cults." MA thesis, Dallas Theological Seminary, 1956.

Trefey, Robert Arthur. *The Theology of Herbert W. Armstrong and Garner T. Armstrong.* Dallas: Dallas Theological Seminary, May, 1968.

BIBLES AND NEW TESTAMENTS

Chamberlain, Roy B. and Herman Feldman. *The Dartsmouth Bible*. Boston: Houghton, 1950.

Fenton, F. *The Holy Bible*. Merrimac: Destiny, 1966.

Friedlander. M. *The Hebrew Bible with English Translation*. Jerusalem: Jerusalem Bible Publishing Co., Ltd., 1953.

Marshall, Alfred. *The Interlinear Greek-English New Testament*. London: Samuel Bagster and Sons, 1959.

The Bible, King James Version.

The Septuagint Version. Grand Rapids: Zondervan, 1970 .

Winter, Ralph D. and Roberta H. Winter. *The Word Study New Testament*. Wheaton: Tyndale House, 1978.

PAMPHLETS, TRACTS

Church of the Covenant. *The Anglo-Saxon Celtic Israel Belief*, Pasadena , California , 1969 .

Modin, J. G. *British-Israel, What Does it Mean?* [n.p.]: [n.n.], [n.d.].

Rand, Howard B. *What is Anglo-Israel Truth?* [n.p.]: [n.n.], [n.d.].

The Messenger of the Covenant. Anglo-Saxon Federation of America, 1928.

PERSONAL CORRESPONDENCE

Letter from John Hutton, Portland, Oregon, September 11, 1980 .

Letter from John Hutton, Portland, Oregon, September 24, 1980 .

Letter from John Hutton, Portland, Oregon, December 10, 1980 .

DATE DUE

			Printed in USA